A HISTORY OF WALLINGFORD VERMONT

Published by

GILBERT HART LIBRARY

JULIAN KLOCK, *Editor*
RUTH BARNARD, *Assistant Editor*
ELEANOR KLOCK, *Assistant Editor*

ACADEMY BOOKS
Rutland, Vermont

PREFACE

"When this work was commenced, we were aware that the accomplishment of our design would be attended with much labor and difficulty. But relying upon the cordial cooperation of our fellow citizens, in affording facilities for the execution of a work, the want and utility of which was universally acknowledged, we were induced to hazard the attempt, by the hope, that we might, in this way, render them at least a trifling service. In the execution of it, we have, however, had to encounter unexpected obstacles, which would probably have deterred us from the undertaking had they been fully anticipated."

The above, written by Zadock Thompson A. B. for the Preface to his Gazetteer of the State of Vermont, published in 1824, expressed our feelings so ably that we could not resist adopting it.

Authentic information concerning the early years was obtained from town records and historical publications. Concerning the last sixty years, or thereabouts, townspeople loaned us their scrapbooks and contributed information on subjects of which they had personal knowledge.

This project was proposed and promoted by Ann Hoadley (Mrs. Francis), Librarian, Gilbert Hart Library. Numerous inquiries at the library for historical information about Wallingford emphasized the need for a comprehensive and up-to-date record to supplement Reverend Walter Thorpe's initial History, published in 1911, and Birney Batcheller's People of Wallingford, published in 1937. Also, this bicentennial year seemed an auspicious time for such a publication.

A list of the many people and organizations who made this History possible by their contributions of money, information, and pictures is included on the following pages.

THE EDITORS

Wallingford
Vermont
March 15, 1976

iii

ACKNOWLEDGEMENTS

Listed below are the names of the Patrons, whose donations made it possible to proceed with the printing of this History. The names are listed in the order in which their donations were received.

Seward Industries
  Roland Q. Seward
Old Stone Shop
  Miss Cornelia Tarbell
Masons
  Chipman Lodge No. 52
Eastern Star
  Waverly Chapter No. 10
Mrs. Edward Kimball
Mrs. Ralph Congdon
Memorial Rotary Club
  of Wallingford, Vermont
Patricia (Underwood) Rothman
Mr. and Mrs. Phillip Blumberg
Mr. and Mrs. James Marquis
Mr. Robert Ittner
Mrs. Ruth Carrier
Mr. and Mrs. Harold Weidman
Mr. and Mrs. Albert Bersaw
Mrs. L. A. Keyes
Lee and Nancy Houghton
Clifford F. Dawson Agency
Mr. and Mrs. Leland Lawson
Blanchard's
  Marvin and Barbara
Dr. and Mrs. Donald Bashaw
Dawson's Inc., Fuel Oil
Hugh and Carolyn Young
  Timber Hill Building Lots
Townsend's Antiques
Mr. and Mrs. Myron Roberts
Mr. and Mrs. Paul Mooney
Fox's Home Bakery

Bicentennial Best Wishes
  from Jorgensen's Honda
Saint Joseph English Language
  Center, Inc.
Mr. and Mrs. Walter R. Beer, Sr.
Wallingford Locker
Mr. and Mrs. Laszlo K. Kerr
The DeSilvey Family
Continental Telephone Company
  of Vermont, Inc.
Fred and Lois Thurlow
Thurlow & Nash Real Estate
Fran and Ann Hoadley
Mr. and Mrs. Charles Gottlieb
Wallingford Gas & Oil
Mr. and Mrs. Ralph E. Stafford
The Fortnightly Club
John and Evelyn (Hoadley) Risher
Mr. and Mrs. J. M. Schippers
Mr. and Mrs. Ashburn Dawson
Elizabeth's Pub
Mr. and Mrs. Wendell Weeks
Mr. and Mrs. Julian Klock
Whitcomb Construction Corp.
Cooperative Fire Insurance
  Association of Vermont
Rowe's General Store
  South Wallingford, Vt.
Mr. and Mrs. Thomas Ketcham
Mr. and Mrs. Edward D. Harwood
Mr. and Mrs. A. J. Kenlan
Wallingford Elementary
  School Staff

White Pigment Corporation
Hearthside Distributors
  East Wallingford, Vt.
Mr. and Mrs. Stanford E. Taylor
Mr. and Mrs. Ralph Lidstone
Pat's Beauty Shop
  Stearns and Pat Stewart
Mr. and Mrs. Albert Perry, Sr.
Francis and Jean (Hoadley)
  Meehan
Maria Wallach
Mr. and Mrs. Sherwin Fish
Mr. and Mrs. William Burke
  Miller
Mr. and Mrs. C. G. Pollock
Mr. and Mrs. C. L. E. Betit
Green Mountain Tea Room
  Herb and Peg Barker,
  South Wallingford, Vt.
Charles and Alice Rist

John H. Blanchard, Sr.
  Excavating & General
  Contracting
Green Hill Homemakers
Ernest and Virginia Downie
Babco Communications
Clinton and Joan Jackson
Walter P. and Nancy M. Kelly
Karl and Gertrude Chapman
Wallingford High School
  Alumni Association
Raymond and Frances Guynup
James and Lynne Gallipo
Towsley's Ceramics
  Boy With The Boot
John H. Macleod
Clayton and Arlene Doty
Mr. and Mrs. L. W. Tucker
Ruth E. Barnard
True Temper Corporation

*   *   *   *

The names of those who contributed information for the History are recorded below. In the process of editing, some of the written information was condensed. However, the complete texts, as submitted, have been filed in the Library and are available for reference.

Alice Rist, Marguerite Cook, Inez Dawson, Karl Chapman, Frank Fox, Roland Seward, Paul Mooney, David Kelley, Mildred D. Lidstone, Bert McClure, Mildred Harwood, Lois Thurlow, William Wedwaldt, Lee Lawson, Robert Eddy, Leona Fish, Gladys Gage, Elmer Hopper, Raymond Bouley, Bertha Savery, Jeannette Eastman, Ann Hoadley.

Madeline Holden, Cornelia Tarbell, Amy Bouley, Clarence Bugbee, David Eaton, Alberta Armstrong, Allyn Seward, Frank Preedom, Doris Wetherby, Helen Witherell, Mabel Stafford, Rhoda Baker, Albert Bersaw, Carolyn Patch, Donald Eddy, Ella Richards, Natalie Congdon, Fred Thurlow, William Parker, Margaret Davenport, Kathleen DeSilvey, Phillip Allison, Orpha Bogert.

Colleen Seaver, Eleanor Davenport, Beatrice Dunham, Nancy Kelly, Virginia Stafford, Madge Miller, Karl Wright, Thomas Miner, Margaret Howley, Roberta Willard, John Macleod, Howard Davison,

Miriam McClure, Betty Fish, Rolland Brown, Frederick Cox, Marlene Dawson, Shirley Graves, Hugh Young, Virginia Austin, Caroline Chase, Helen Weidman, Natalie MacIntyre.

William Dolt, Louise Adams, Beatrice Baker, Ruth Carrier, Mildred Ward, Thomas Stafford, Joy Millard, Emma Towsley, Thelma Perry, Albert Perry, Harriet Gilman, Clifford Willard, Guy Stafford, Patricia Towsley, Lynn Hebert, Sanford Witherell, Donald Shedd, Kenneth Fish, Marguerite Houghton, Sherwin Fish, Lee Houghton, Rev. Raymond Walsh.

Lois Randolph, J. A. Taylor, Doris Dolt, Sandra Marquis, Loretta Townsend, Anna Mooney, Constance Bashaw, Florence Fox, Hazel Lawson, Stephen Maranville, Elizabeth Ketcham, Stanford Taylor, John Zecher, James McCann, Lynne Gallipo, Ralph Lidstone, Homer Dawson, Rev. Richard Armstrong, Philip Stephan.

*   *   *   *

Pictures have been supplied by Donald Wiedenmayer, Helen and Sanford Witherell, Bert McClure, Alice Rist, Ann Hoadley, Esther Thomas Ridlon, William Roberts, Frank Fox, Karl Chapman, Mildred Ward, Carolyn Patch, Anna Mooney, Doris Wetherby, Colleen Seaver, John Risher, Wilbur Marquis, Ann Pratt, Beatrice Dunham, Leona Fish, Harriet Gilman, Kelley Young, Rotary Club of Wallingford, Holly Young. Illustrations also were printed from glass plates taken by the late Birney Batcheller and found at the Library. The drawing of the Library was made by Natalie MacIntyre and given to the Library.

CONTENTS

Road along Otter Creek, by Birney Batcheller

Chapter 1

The Land and Its Uses

When the land that is now the town of Wallingford was Indian country, it was uninhabited; it was a hunting ground, and occasionally a battle ground, for the Algonquins and the Iroquois. As colonists began coming to America, it was still disputed territory that was claimed by both England and France. Then in 1760, when peace came following the French defeat in Canada, it and all the land that is now Vermont looked much more attractive to settler and speculator alike.

On November 27, 1761, Governor Benning Wentworth of New Hampshire granted to Captain Eliakim Hall and 63 associates 23,040 acres in a tract roughly six miles square, "for the due encouragement of settling a new Plantation within our said Province." The "new Plantation" was to be named Wallingford after the town in Connecticut where most of the grantees lived. Six miles square was chosen for the size of a town, it is said, because from anywhere within that area the distance to market, to church, or to town meeting could be travelled between morning and evening chores.

In 1764, the Connecticut River was officially designated New York's eastern boundary, settling an old dispute with New Hampshire, and putting Captain Hall's grant under New York's jurisdiction. He and a number of the grantees immediately applied to New York for a patent confirming their New Hampshire charter. It is said that the Governor and Council of New York approved the patent in 1767, but that it was never issued, because of the increasing turmoil that was to bring on the Revolutionary War.

The proprietors met in 1772, in Wallingford, Connecticut, to organize the new town, and early in 1773 for the first drawing of lots. The lots, 100 acres each, were surveyed and markers set up between 1773 and 1795. The first settler with title to his land, Abraham Jackson, arrived with his family during the summer of 1773, and others, mostly from Connecticut, followed. The town's population had reached 536 by 1790, the date of the first census.

For the most part, because of foresight, luck, or location, Wallingford was free from the land controversies that are a part of the history and folklore of early Vermont. There was some difficulty near the original boundary with Clarendon because of tracts sold in that area by John Lydius, who claimed the Otter Creek valley by purchase from the Indians and a grant from the Massachusetts Bay colony. Adjustments were made in the boundary, resulting in an irregular line between Wallingford and Clarendon. The conflicts which involved Wallingford seem to have been quickly settled, but controversy in Clarendon continued until after Vermont had declared its independence. It was finally settled when a "Quieting Act" was passed by the Legislature.

In 1781, Abraham Jackson, Jr., and 29 others obtained from the Legislature a grant of land east of Wallingford, called Jackson's Gore or Wallingford Gore. Several of these Wallingford settlers moved from the area near Otter Creek to the eastern part of town and the Gore. Tradition has it that they sold their land on the Creek for a shilling an acre, and moved east to higher ground to get away from the flies and mosquitoes. In 1792 this Gore, along with 3388 acres from Wallingford and acreage from Ludlow, became the town of Mount Holly. The next year the Legislature passed an act transferring land on West Hill from Tinmouth to Wallingford.

Both of these land transfers had previously been considered by Wallingford voters at a town meeting. On October 8, 1792, according to the record, "a number of inhabitants of Tinmouth requested to be set off to this town, the vote was called and passed in the negative. Then after some arguments, motion was made to reconsider said vote. Voted to reconsider it. Then voted to adjourn to the 10th October. . . ." On October 10th. . . . "a motion was made to try the mind whether they were willing to have the east part of Tinmouth annexed to this town. Voted in the affirmative. Then a committee from Jackson's Gore requested to be set off as a separate town and to have one mile off the east part of this town annexed to them for the time being. The vote was passed in the affirmative." The net result of these two votes was to move Wallingford's boundaries about a mile west, and to slightly increase its size. The Vermont Year Book presently gives the town's area as 24,621 acres.

The lay of the land had much to do with how the town developed. The mountains and valleys, the many rocks and hills, abundant springs and water courses, all influenced the settlers in their choice of location. Many chose first the fairly level land of the Otter Creek valley; others went to the higher ground in the west, or east beyond the mountains. John Hopkins was on West Hill in 1770, Abraham Jackson and Abraham Ives in Wallingford village in 1773, Amasa and Ebenezer and Joel Hart in the central part of town before 1775. According to a note in a Kent genealogy, Elias Kent in 1803 "bought a lot near the summit of one of the high hills in the east part of the town, then a wilderness, and plying his axe to the stately timber with a will soon had quite an opening, and his first house was of logs covered with bark."

All of the land was forest. There was game of all kinds—deer, bear, beaver—and fish in the lakes and streams. Once a settler had cut down

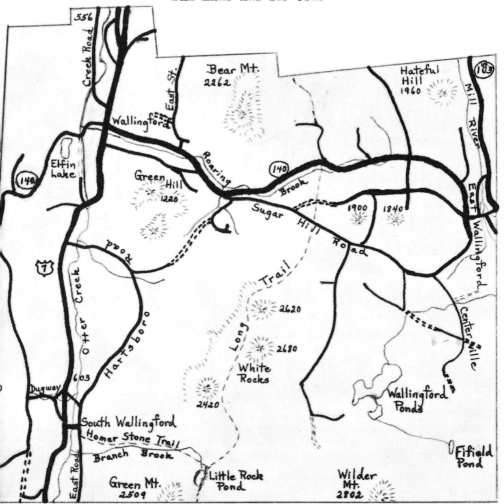

*Wallingford Township. Traced from Town highway and U. S.
Geological Survey maps.*

trees and built his log house, he burned the timber and brush, and planted
corn and wheat as best he could among the stumps. He raised flax and
acquired a few sheep. His taxes could be paid in grain; and for a cash
crop he might make potash or pearl ash from the ashes of the wood he
had burned.

In her book, *Vermont Tradition,* Dorothy Canfield wrote, "It
took a great deal of time and a great deal of hard work to transform a
big elm tree into five tons of wood, then to burn the wood into ashes,
then to extract the lye from the ashes and thence, by evaporation, to

produce 39 pounds of potash." Potash was light in comparison to its value, and could be transported easily. A pound of potash had a much greater cash value than a pound of wheat. And there was a ready market for potash in England, where it was needed for the manufacture of textiles and soap. So the settler could sell or trade the potash for things he could not make, or raise, or otherwise get from the land, such as powder, shot, salt, or tea.

The market for potash dwindled after 1810, as sodium made from salt was substituted in industry for the more expensive potash. By this time, the era of the self-sufficient farmer was about over. Roads were being made, and commerce and industry began to develop—blacksmith shops, tanneries, stores, and mills of various kinds run by water power.

The first inhabitants of the township tended to settle in neighborhoods. Wallingford village, with water power sites on both Roaring Brook and Otter Creek, was the first. By 1820 it had mills, shops, and about forty houses along its one north and south street. South Wallingford, with its water power, veins of marble, and good farm land, also developed early. Some spoke of the two villages as North Wallingford and South Wallingford. Hartsboro was a cluster of farms, a school, and a sawmill south of Green Hill. There were farms on Sugar Hill in the east central part of town, with a school, a store, and a "common" church (used in turn by Baptists, Congregationalists, and Methodists) as the center. Forest Hill, near the Mount Holly border, included farms and the hamlet of Centerville. The first settler in the neighborhood of East Wallingford arrived in 1812; most of that village's growth was to come some years later. In the 1880's Aldrichville, a lumbering camp, would develop and thrive for just a few years near Little Rock Pond.

Farming was for many years the chief occupation in the town, but the emphasis shifted with changing conditions. Sheep farming, for which the climate was well suited, increased during the early 1800's. The sheep that the settlers had brought with them were the ordinary kind, healthy and coarse-wooled. Merinos, with fine soft wool, began to be imported into the country in 1801. In 1814, Isaac Munson acquired a Merino ram that cost $1500, to upgrade his flock of 165 sheep. In 1827, Deacon Button of Clarendon went twice to Connecticut to buy some of these Merinos, and the second time David Holden of Wallingford went with him, and bought a few for himself. Dyer Townsend, who is said to have had for many years the best flock of Merinos in the state, bought his first animals from Deacon Button. Alfred Hull also had a large flock. Sheep raising for the wool, which found a ready market in Boston and other cities, and sheep breeding, flourished until after the Civil War. The census reported more than 4,000 sheep in the town in 1850, 2,000 in 1860, fewer than 1,000 in 1870. In 1974, there were 9.

Centerville 1890-1895

As the number of sheep decreased, there was a shift to dairy farming which has continued to the present time. In the early days, little fresh milk was sold; what the family did not use was made into cheese or butter on the farm. Around 1860 cheese factories were started and surplus milk was taken there. Alvin Hawkins was farming on Sugar Hill in the 1880's, and is believed to have built the first silo in Rutland County. He had a cheese factory, bought milk from neighboring farms, and returned the whey for the farmers to feed to their pigs. After the invention of the milk separator in 1874, creameries began to replace the cheese factories and received an increasing share of the farmers' milk. By 1930, no farm-made butter or cheese was coming to market, and almost all of the milk was being brought to the creameries.

In 1849, a railroad was built from Rutland to Bellows Falls. The line went through a corner of Wallingford, perhaps because someone had discovered during the old days of stage coaching that the best place south of Montpelier to cross the Green Mountains was in neighboring Mount Holly. In 1852, another line was built in the Otter Creek valley, from Rutland to Troy, and passing through Wallingford and South Wallingford villages. This improved transportation had a great impact on both farming and industry in the town, opening up new markets, but also bringing in competing products. Its coming was a spur to the growth of East Wallingford, but a blow to South Wallingford, which had been a stage-coach stop. Its coming also started the mining of gravel from the long strip of land west of Wallingford and of Otter Creek, which is still going on. A branch of the railroad crossed the Creek not far from the station so that gravel trains could bring the material out from what used to be called the Sand Bank.

By the end of the town's first century, around 1870, most of the usable land had been settled, and a network of roads connected the settlements. These roads were considered important, as shown by entries in the town's records. March 10, 1778 it was voted that A. Jackson, also Joseph Jackson and Abraham Ives "inspect into the matter of highways." In April, 1778, "voted that every man shall work 3 days on the road." Specifications for roads included the width, sometimes 3 rods, sometimes 4; one mentioned in 1828 was to "be cleared of timber and under Brush said width and that said road shall be worked suitable for travelling with Carriages at least 18 feet." By that date, county roads and county road commissioners are being mentioned. And each volume of the old records of town meetings has surveys of roads that are being opened up or rerouted.

The population of the town increased pretty steadily, reaching a peak of 2023 in 1870, according to census figures. The second century reversed this trend; population decreased gradually to 1865 people in 1880, 1733 in 1890, and the network of roads began to shrink a little. Hill land, that could provide its owner a good livelihood when it was new, and when all of the work was done by the family and the animals, could not compete with the new level lands in the mid-western states, tilled and harvested by machines, or with Australia when it came to sheep raising. And the game was about gone, because of over-hunting and the clearing of the forest. Families began to move from the hill farms, and the decline in the town's population continued.

The acreage of land in farms fell from 23,000 in 1850, to just over 18,000 in 1935; the decline has continued. The number of farms is lower, too; South Wallingford had 28 at one time, of which one was left in 1974; there were 14 on West Hill in 1916, and there are none now. The largest number for the entire town was 206 in 1860; now there are no more than a dozen or so, depending on how a farm is defined. The number of farm animals is also much smaller. Cattle numbered 2,400 in 1880, 900 last year; horses 300 in 1880, 60 in 1974. Humpy and Dippy, driven by Roy Fuller, were the last oxen in Wallingford village, around 1915, and Harry Dawson had the last pair on Sugar Hill. Almost 2000 hens were owned in 1880, last year the listers found only 70. A couple of geese are known to live in the town, but there are no more peacocks; years ago one of the Munson families south of Wallingford village kept them, and more

Lumbering at Aldrichville

recently the Saffords also had them. When their squawking was heard, carried on a south wind, it was a sign to the villagers of coming rain.

Trees were cut from the time the earliest settlers arrived, at first mostly to clear the land. After roads and transportation had developed, forest products were an important part of the town's economy. Pulpwood was cut on Sugar Hill and above South Wallingford, and lumber in the eastern part of town especially. The largest single operation was at Aldrichville, near Little Rock Pond and north of it. Barney and Edgar Aldrich, who had a lumber and chair-stock business in East Wallingford, made a number of purchases and leases of timberland in the southeastern part of town, the first in 1879, and the largest, over 2000 acres, in 1894. A sawmill was built, and then log houses and a log schoolhouse were provided for the lumberjacks and their families, and a boarding house was built for the single men. Twenty-eight pupils attended the school, some of them starting at age 4, and they were taught by 16-year-old Eva Edgerton.

The camp was in virgin forest, and the size of the timber was impressive, for instance, trees cut for derrick poles 74' long, and 2,800 feet of lumber sawed from one birch tree. Later, the sawmill was moved to South Wallingford, near the railroad tracks. The other buildings on the mountain were left for hunters or whoever might want to use them. An article written in 1932 stated that when one of the owners returned to the old site some years after it was abandoned, he found the buildings burned to the ground. All that remained of Aldrichville was a huge sawdust pile.

As farming declined in the hills, uses of the land changed. The increasing number of automobiles also had an influence. Some farm homes continued to be year-round homes, with the fields rented to neighboring farmers or allowed to grow up to forest again, and the owners driving to jobs in town. Some were sold to "summer people" who drove up from the metropolitan areas to the south. A number of homes on West Hill were remodelled, some of them handsomely, as vacation homes. Starting around 1920, cottages were built near Elfin Lake, which was formerly called Fox Pond, so that the southwest corner of the town is something of a summer colony.

The name Fox Pond and the ownership of the land bordering the lake relate to early Wallingford history. William Fox served in the Revolutionary War, farmed in Tinmouth, then in 1791 bought a farm in Wallingford. Other parcels of land were purchased, and he finally owned much of the land south and west of the lake, which became known as Fox Pond, and was so designated on early maps. There has been considerable interest in the change of name to Elfin Lake, but no satisfactory explanation. One old-timer, who still calls it Fox Pond, says that it was changed when someone just got la-di-da. The earliest written reference to Elfin Lake that has been found is in a brochure published by the New Wallingford Hotel around 1893. As for the land on the east side, that too harks back to an early settler. Solomon Miller of West Springfield, Mass., began buying land in Wallingford in 1784, and by the time he came here in 1787 he owned the southern half of what is now Walling-ford village; Church Street was laid out across his property. His son Alexander inherited, bought, and sold land; he gave the plot for the Congregational Church. Part of his property, including land along the lake, was bequeathed to his son-in-law, Elias Wheaton Kent, who be-queathed it to his daughter, Lucretia Kent Stone, who in 1919 gave thirty acres of it to the people of Wallingford for a park.

The new developments—the park, the cottages on the west side, and a boy's camp built in the late 1920's—naturally changed conditions at the lake. Before 1920, it had been a quiet place of woods and water. There was a little swimming at the one natural beach at the south end, some fishing, a little boating, and occasionally a cow stepping in for a drink of water down at the south-west corner. In winter, however, it was perhaps quieter even after the developments than in the old days, with no more ice harvests and the shift in winter sports from skating to skiing.

The very northwest corner of the town is practically wilderness. Perhaps it always was, as none of the old maps found show any roads or dwellings in the area. But there are holes that look like cellar holes, and one old deed has a reference to the King's Highway, so perhaps it was sparsely settled and then abandoned very early.

The northeast part seems not to have changed very much over the years. Bear Mountain is rough country, lumbered periodically by private interests. On either side of the mountain are less hilly sections that are thinly populated, one along East Street, and another west of Mill River.

A different kind of development has taken place in the southeast area of the town. The Green Mountain National Forest, owned and operated by the U. S. Forest Service, covers 7387 acres, roughly 30% of the land in the township. As a Forest Service bulletin states, "The Vermont General Assembly passed an enabling act in 1925 inviting the U. S. Forest Service to establish a National Forest here. The purpose was then, and is today, to establish and maintain a healthy, vigorous forest which will protect the quality of mountain streams and provide a continuous supply of forest products and services." In this forest area "campers, hunters, hikers, fishermen, and recreationists of all kinds enjoy their pursuits amid scenic beauty unrivalled in the eastern states."

Land in the National Forest is not taxable and so each town with land in the Forest area receives, by law, a certain part of the revenue from forest operations in lieu of taxes. The amount of the total revenue, and that received by each town, fluctuates considerably from year to year, because it depends on the total amount and price of the timber cut throughout the entire Green Mountain Forest. Income is also received from ski area permits and other use fees; permits to cut firewood, however, are free. The revenue each town receives is based on the percentage of forest area in that town to the total forest area. Wallingford received $4,452.16 in 1973 and $2,782.42 in 1974. Within the boundaries of the Forest, there is also some privately owned land, which continues on the town's tax rolls. Before any of this land can be sold or donated to the Forest, the transfer must be approved by the Selectmen.

A number of natural features are included in Wallingford's part of the Green Mountain National Forest. White Rocks is a prominent landmark that was mentioned in all of the old histories, as were the Ice Beds at its foot. Wallingford Pond, also called Hiram Pond, Big Pond, or Spectacle Pond because of its shape, and Little Rock Pond, popular with hikers, are near the town's southern border. The Long Trail and the White Rocks Picnic Area are other attractions.

The Picnic Area, reached by the old Sugar Hill Road, was opened in June, 1937, by the Forest Service, and expanded in 1957. Ample parking space has been provided, a 90-foot well drilled to supply water to the area, and toilets built. The trees have been thinned out to make a very pleasant picnic place, carpeted with pine needles and equipped with stone fireplaces and picnic tables with benches. From the picnic area there are three trails, one to the top of the cliff, one to the hill that used to be called Peter Cook's Knoll, and one to the Ice Beds.

The Long Trail—"a footpath in the wilderness"—passes over the summits of the main range of the Green Mountains between the Massachusetts and Canadian borders. The Green Mountain Club was organized and the Trail begun in 1910; the Manchester-Killington section that passes through Wallingford was opened in 1917. It goes past Little Rock Pond, crosses the site of Aldrichville, Homer Stone Brook, and the old South Wallingford-Wallingford Pond Road. The Homer Stone Trail that goes down the mountain to South Wallingford follows this old road part of the way. The main trail goes over the top of White Rocks, with a short spur to the brink of the cliff where there is an exceptional view. Just beyond, the Keewaydin Trail branches off; it leads to the White Rocks Picnic Area less than a mile away. After the White Rocks summit, the Trail goes on across Sugar Hill, across the Gulf Road, and between Bear Mountain and Button Hill toward Spring Lake in Shrewsbury.

The Forest Service maintains the part of the Trail that is in the Green Mountain National Forest, and the Green Mountain Club the rest. For a time, a Wallingford Scout troop was responsible for the Keewaydin Trail. In the early years of the Trail, much of the maintenance consisted of just keeping it open. But traffic has increased so that now maintenance also includes relocating or repairing sections of the Trail that have been over-used. On a pleasant summer day, a hiker will meet as many people on the Trail as he would on a village street.

The trend of declining year-round population in the rural areas has not carried over to the villages. When a 1955 map that shows roads and buildings is compared with a similar map for 1894, very little change is indicated for those years in East and South Wallingford. Wallingford village, however, grew during that time, and has continued to grow in the years since 1955. Prospect Street was opened up around 1914. (A special item in the 1915 Town Report noted that W. P. Cary paid part of the cost of building this street, which crossed his land.) Taft Terrace was developed in 1947, Nash Drive in 1959, Shedd Place in the 1960's, and existing streets and roads have more houses. The 1973 town highway map notes an estimated population of 886 in the "urban compact," which is the village and its immediate environs; the town's population in 1970 was 1676.

There are several planned developments on the outskirts of the village. The first, Highland Homesites, was laid out in 1958 on meadow land of the former Thayer farm, between Elm Street Extension and Route 140, and adjacent to the north end of Elfin Lake, where a beach and tennis courts have been constructed. John Macleod planned it for 30 vacation homes, of which 15 have been built by out-of-state families; there are two year-round homes having resident owners.

Hugh and Carolyn Young call their development Timber Hill Estates; it is on the former Hopkins farm and Green Hill, off SouthMain Street. The first street, Deerfield Drive, was established in 1962 and has five houses; in 1974 a larger area, with several roads and sites for 22 homes, was added.

Sherwin and Leona Fish have opened up an area overlooking the village on the east, reached by Hillside Road which branches off upper School Street. The land is from the former Myron Kelley farm, there is a spring-fed pond, and village water and sewer have been put in. The Fish's ranch-type house and three others have been built, and there is room for expansion.

Church Hill Knolls, begun in the spring of 1973, consists of approximately 30 acres where Dr. Cootey had his camp, on the south side of Church Street near the top of the hill. The owners, Fred and Lois Thurlow, have subdivided the property into 17 lots with a five-acre plot

1927 Flood
Depot Street, Wallingford

set aside for recreation. There is one development out in the country a mile southwest of East Wallingford, about 200 acres planned by an out-of-town group, Land-vest, for 14 large lots and called Highridge.

Any region that has both hills and abundant water is likely to experience floods, as Wallingford has. One of the worst occurred in November, 1927, when more than 8″ of rain, the amount of precipitation expected in two months, fell in 36 hours. An interview reported in the *Rutland Herald* described how George Kelley was delivering mail on West Hill the first morning of the rain, where "sheets of water were flowing down the hillsides, landslides were blocking mountain roads, and streams were washing out roads and carrying away bridges. By the Peattie's summer home a waterfall blocked the way, but he managed to turn his horse and cart. Baker Brook was running, a foaming mass, nearly up to his horse's body, where the road had been. He couldn't go that way. In his high rubber boots, with whip-stock to sound the water, he walked on the edge of grass which had once lined the road and led his horse through the seething water." He did reach South Wallingford safely, but mail service was not back to normal until the resumption of train service two weeks later. Route 7 was flooded both north and south of Wallingford village, part of the Gulf Road was washed out, and Roaring Brook did more damage in the village as it overflowed its banks and found new channels.

At the time of the 1938 hurricane, Mill River flooded and did considerable damage in East Wallingford, changing course to form an island where none had been before, and washing away the house and garden of the station agent, Mr. W. A. Train. In 1973, a flood on June 30, damaged the Dugway and other roads near South Wallingford and part of the Sugar Hill Road. In East Wallingford, the bridge over Freeman Brook went out and has not been replaced; instead, a 500′ road extension to Route 103 has been built.

More changes in the town's roads have followed changed land use and the increased number of cars. The least travelled have been discontinued or have become trails, as in the National Forest. Some have been rerouted to avoid the steepest hills, as was done as far back as 1875, when the old road to Tinmouth was abandoned and the present Route 140 up West Hill was built; parts of this road have been rebuilt or relocated since then. In East Wallingford village, the road was rerouted in 1910 and a bridge built over the railroad to eliminate a grade crossing. Now that there are few trains, the bridge is gone and the old road is back in service; when necessary, cars are stopped at the crossing by a flagman from the infrequent trains.

The roads that climbed the hills had ditches at the sides, and water bars at intervals in the steepest parts. As the name indicates, these were

Railroad Street, Wallingford

River Street, East Wallingford

East Road, South Wallingford

to divert into the ditches the water flowing down the road and washing it out, especially in the spring. They were also useful to horse-drawn vehicles because the driver could rest his horse, with the wheels of his vehicle braked somewhat by the packed earth of the bar. But they were bad for cars, and have generally been eliminated.

The main roads, Route 7 and the short section of Route 103 through East Wallingford, have gradually been widened and straightened. Route 7 is divided for a bit where it enters the town at the north, and has a railroad overpass at the south end of the village, built in 1937. Between Wallingford and South Wallingford the road level has been raised as it passes through the low parts where the water meadows flood each spring. A great deal of work was done on the Gulf Road in the 1920's. These, of course, are state highways, which the town now has instead of the county roads of the early days. Mileage of state highways is 16.66 miles, of state-aid highways, 3.86 miles, and of town roads, 40.6 miles, for a total of 61.12 miles of road in the town.

The straightening of Route 7 made streets of its cut-off curves, Pine Drive and Old Route 7 in Wallingford, and Tuckaway Lane, where the Dugway goes up West Hill near South Wallingford. At least two streets are the stumps of abandoned roads: Cook Drive south of Wallingford village was the beginning of the old road to Tinmouth, and Hull Avenue formerly went all the way to East Street, where one can still see a lane that was its other end.

Some rather interesting changes of street names have been noted in old histories and on old maps. In South Wallingford, the East Road was once called Stovepipe Avenue. In Wallingford, Hull Avenue was often called Stafford Avenue, School Street was Central Street before the school was built in 1865, and Elm Street was Mill Street in its early days. A single mention was found of Railroad Street as Mechanics Street, of Circular Avenue as Lime Kiln Street, and of the section of Creek Road just beyond the factory as Evergreen Avenue. And old timers still think of Florence Avenue as Lover's Lane.

Sometimes a change has represented a return to an earlier condition, as with the cleared land that is gradually returning to forest. In Centerville, a former barnyard is now a grove of maples. Coming down West Hill, one no longer sees the valley spread out below, and the lake, because growth along Route 140 has cut off the view. And the animals, almost all gone a hundred years ago, are back. Around 1880 a few deer were brought into the county and no hunting was allowed for a time until they established themselves. Since then, with improved habitat and controlled hunting, the deer herd is once again sizable. There are beavers now, and a few otters, plenty of muskrats, woodchucks, and raccoons, but these last may have been here right along. A coyote was found in the town recently, something new for this part of the country. The bird population, too, has some new members. Cardinals, mockingbirds, and titmice, all southern birds, have moved into the area because so many people have bird feeders.

*   *   *   *

In looking back over the 200 years of Wallingford's history, change seems to be the most appropriate word, the word that sums it all up. The old cellar holes and the stone walls in the midst of forest trees are reminders of a way of life that is gone. And in some cases a good thing. The settler who sold his potash did not know—few knew then—that he was robbing his soil. The early farmer did not realize that pasturing sharp-nosed, sharp-hoofed sheep on a steep hillside was an invitation to erosion. Modern agriculture not only manages the land better but is more productive, and a diversified economy allows more choice in how land is used. We can expect that change will continue into the future. Questions now waiting for answers—where to have a landfill, what to do about a worn-out bridge, how to control development in the public interest—are signs of changes that will surely come.

Chapter 2

In The Old Days

What one considers to be "old days" depends upon how old one is. For the purposes of this history, the old days are any time before the Great Depression of the early 1930's.

It required almost all of the time and energy of the first settlers to provide just the basic necessities of life—food, clothing, and shelter. They provided food by farming, hunting, trapping, and fishing. From wool and flax the women spun the thread and wove the cloth needed to make clothes and blankets. The first shelters built were log cabins.

The type of building which followed the log cabin is described in the *History of Rutland County* as "a house of one story, a huge chimney in the middle, surrounded by a kitchen, two square rooms off the kitchen, and an entryway between the latter rooms."

By the early 1800's some of the big fine houses of Wallingford were built. In a number of these old homes the best room, commonly called the parlor, was located on the north side of the house. It was reserved mostly for special occasions such as weddings, funerals, and entertaining guests. One reason given for having this room on the north and least pleasant side of the house was to keep the sun from fading the carpet. These houses had no central heating, electric lights, electric appliances, or flush toilets.

Water was obtained from numerous springs throughout the town, or from wells. Each of the three villages had one or more privately owned water systems which provided running water to a number of homes. Several of these systems still serve a few houses today.

Because metal pipe was not available, suitable conduit was made from logs. This was done by boring a hole lengthwise with an auger, made by a blacksmith. Then one end of the log was tapered to fit into a cone-shaped recess in the end of the next log. These were called "pump logs," and were joined together to make a conduit of any length desired. About 1876 the wooden conduit was replaced by welded iron pipe. To bring the water into the house, an iron pump was used and generally installed by the kitchen sink.

Spring water is likely to be hard water, so in some homes rain water was collected to use for laundry. An eavestrough was installed at the edge of the roof, and the rainwater piped either into a cistern in the house or into a big rain barrel with a cover outside the house. The phrase from the old song, "shout down my rain barrel," referred to the echo that one could hear in an almost empty barrel; and of course "slide down my cellar door" meant sliding down the slanting cover of the hatchway or outside entrance to the cellar, common in those days when produce would be brought in and stored in the cellar for winter use.

The houses were heated by wood burned in fireplaces. The big houses might have anywhere from three to six of them. These fireplaces were shallow so the maximum amount of heat would be reflected into the room, and had a wide hearth so the coals could not tumble out onto the floor. Wood stoves replaced the fireplaces in many cases. Later on came central heating from a furnace burning either wood or coal.

In pioneer days, cooking was done at a wide fireplace which had a swinging crane on one side from which kettles were hung over the fire. Later, this was supplanted by the kitchen range, which had an oven and also a reservoir on the side for heating water. It took considerable experience and skill to obtain and hold the proper oven temperature with a wood fire. In those days, children were kept busy doing chores; one often assigned was filling the woodbox.

Kitchen fireplace with crane and kettles, Stafford-Klock house

Lighting was first by candle and next by kerosene lamp. It was not until 1908, or thereabouts, that electric light and power was available. There were a few street lights in Wallingford village, kerosene lights set on posts. At one time Frank Preedom was lamplighter for his neighborhood, where each of the families had "chipped in" five gallons of kerosene. He had a small stepladder to reach the lamp, and a can of kerosene. He would put in just enough oil to keep the light burning for a specified time. If some of the neighbors let him know that they were going to be out late, he would put in more than the usual amount of oil.

In these old days before the telephone, the stores in Wallingford village had a delivery man with a horse and wagon, who took orders and made deliveries to regular customers. Arthur Cobb was delivery man for H. G. Savery; in his wagon he had a huge orange umbrella, like those used at the seashore, to protect him from sun and rain; it was installed permanently, the handle fastened to the wagon seat. Then on certain days, say Wednesdays and Saturdays, George Ladabouche would drive along the street with an enclosed wagon, equipped with a scale, and sell meat. You would watch for him if you wanted any. Fish was sometimes sold in the same way.

A number of village families, especially the larger ones, kept a cow. For the many who didn't, Andrew Bartholomew, a milkman, delivered milk daily. Because not all homes had a way to keep it cool, and unpasteurized milk turned sour quickly in hot weather, it might be delivered twice a day in the summer. Milk tickets were bought in advance. When you wanted milk, you put a container by the front door, along with one or more pint tickets. The milkman then measured into your container the amount of milk indicated by the tickets.

Within the memory of older residents, cattle were sometimes driven down Wallingford's Main Street. In an earlier time, long drives were not unusual; driving a flock of sheep to market might take a week or more.

One girl from East Wallingford who came to Wallingford to live with relatives while she went to high school, brought her Jersey cow, Buttercup, with her. This was done because she wasn't to drink "bought" milk. (At that time people were just beginning to realize the importance of testing cows for tuberculosis, routine now but not then; three local youngsters had contracted bovine tuberculosis.) Also, it provided the relatives with extra milk and cream in return for her board and room. She went home for the weekend by train, by way of Rutland, using a mileage book; this had, between its cardboard covers, a long strip of paper marked off in divisions, one for each mile travelled, and the conductor tore off the proper number to pay for the journey.

There were ice boxes in most homes, until the late 1920's when domestic electric refrigerators began to replace them in large numbers.

Use of commercial refrigeration on a large scale occurred later. An ice box had to be refilled every few days, depending on the weather, at a cost of about 5 or 10 cents. You put a card in the window (ICE) if you needed any, and the "ice man" would deliver and put in the box the size cake that was needed. As the ice melted, the water dripped into a pan under the ice box, and this had to be emptied daily.

Farmers usually had a pond from which they cut ice each winter. Also, in each village there were ice houses where ice was stored, packed in sawdust for insulation. The Whiting Milk Company of Boston had ice houses in Wallingford and South Wallingford, so railroad cars carrying milk could be refrigerated. Ice for Wallingford was harvested on Fox Pond (Elfin Lake). It was sawed into cakes which generally were about 12 x 24 x 10 inches, and would weigh at least 100 pounds.

When farming was the chief occupation, it was the custom to have "husking bees." After the corn was cut it was stacked in shocks at the field and left there for a few days to dry out. Then it would be drawn to the barn for husking in the afternoon, and each farmer would ask his friends and neighbors to help. While the men and older boys and girls husked the corn, the women folk were busy preparing a hearty meal. After supper there would be a barn dance, to conclude a day when a good time was had by all.

South Main Street, Wallingford

In the early 1900's the dirt roads and village streets were narrow compared to what they are today, and were dusty. In Wallingford village, John Wood used to stand out in front of his store the first thing each morning in the summertime and hose down the four corners (Main, Depot, and School Streets). Later on, the town put calcium chloride on the principal streets to lay the dust.

Horse-drawn sleds and sleighs were used in winter, so the roads were not plowed; in fact, snow was shovelled on any bare spots. An item in the Town Report of 1911 reads, "Snowing bridge—$1.00"; snow was put on the roadway planking of the covered bridge so that sleds and sleighs could pass through easily. The sidewalks were plowed. Joe Pelkey used to get up at 3:30 in the morning and, with a horse-drawn plow, clear the sidewalks for those who worked at the shop—they all walked to work then. Mr. Pelkey is said to have whistled while he was plowing, and some people complained that he was causing a disturbance by whistling so early in the morning.

In 1937, Main Street was widened and paved with concrete. Now, Main Street is part of U. S. Route 7, is two lanes wide, paved with blacktop, and maintained by the state. In winter it is plowed and salted to keep the road from becoming icy and slippery. Most of the splendid elms and maples which used to line Main Street are gone, because of Dutch elm disease, old age, and the effects of the wide pavement and the salt. In recent years, young maples and flowering crabs have been

School Street, East Wallingford

planted in lawns bordering on the street so that it won't look so bare in the future.

Rev. H. H. Sanderson, in an address at the Centennial of Wallingford in 1873, said, ". . . perhaps no greater change has taken place since the days of our fathers than in the modes of conveyance. For our grandfathers and grandmothers did not use to ride in Pullman cars and beautiful covered topped carriages . . . The ordinary mode of passing from place to place was on horseback." Looking from our vantage point of today, by far the more significant of the changes mentioned by Mr. Sanderson was the railroad Pullman car.

Train service for East Wallingford began in 1849 on the Rutland and Burlington Railroad, and for Wallingford and South Wallingford in 1852 on the Western Vermont Railroad. Both of these became parts of the Rutland Railroad.

When completed, the Rutland Railroad ran from Ogdensburg, New York, across to Alburg, Vermont, and then down to Rutland. At Rutland it divided, with the western branch going to Chatham, New York, and the eastern branch to Bellows Falls. By connecting railroads, through trains ran to Montreal, Boston, and New York City.

The first steam locomotives burned wood and required large quantities of water. Trains stopped at South Wallingford for wood, and for water either there or at Wallingford where there was also a railroad water tank. The book on the Rutland Railroad by Jim Shaughnessy, on page 46, shows a picture of a locomotive converted to coal in 1888, so it is assumed that coal was used from that time until steam locomotives were replaced by diesels around 1950.

Passenger service was good. In 1930, there were eight passenger trains daily, including a sleeper. Some were locals which stopped at all stations, and there were also the Green Mountain Flyers, which stopped at fewer stations. Special trains were run on occasion; for example, during the "World's Fair" at South Wallingford, a special train let passengers off at a nearby crossing so they could walk to the fair grounds.

For several years around 1906 to 1910, liquor could not be sold in Wallingford but was readily available in Rutland. Therefore, the fact that the north-bound flyer ordinarily did not stop here on Saturday afternoon temporarily caused some concern to a few residents, because the train was their only available means of transportation. However, it was soon discovered that the train would stop at Wallingford to pick up passengers for Rouses Point and beyond. So those feeling the need to go to Rutland for a drink would pool their resources and buy one ticket to Rouses Point plus as many additional tickets as needed to Rutland. The Saturday evening train south stopped here regularly, so the return trip presented no problem other than to be sure to get on it.

Train No. 64 going south. Cars in the train are refrigerator car, mail car, baggage car, smoking car, passenger car, diner, observation car.

Express, freight, and mail service was provided by the railroad. Mail was picked up at stations along the way, sorted in the mail car, pouched, transferred to another train if necessary, and ultimately dropped off at its destination. The station master at Wallingford trundled the mail to the station (the present fire station was the railroad station), put it on the mail car, and took the bag of incoming mail, which had been tossed off the train, back to the post office. At smaller stations, such as Wallingford, where the flyers did not stop, the outgoing mail bag was suspended from a cross-arm on a pole close to the track. On each door of the mail car there was a hinged arm-like device which was extended to catch the mail bag in the middle and haul it in as the train went by.

A milk train, with all ice-refrigerated cars, ran daily from Ogdensburg, New York, to Rutland, picking up cans of milk from stations along the way. At Rutland, the train was divided into two sections; one section continued on to Chatham, New York, and New York City, and the other went to Bellows Falls and Boston. As many as 100 to 150 forty-quart cans of milk were shipped daily from the creamery here at Wallingford, and the milk cars were refrigerated with ice harvested from Fox Pond. The cars went from here to Rutland, where they were added to the milk train section going to Boston. In the same way, milk was shipped from East Wallingford to Boston.

As a result of improved highways, and increased use of passenger cars, busses, trucks, tank cars, and moving vans, traffic on the railroad decreased drastically. By 1952 there were only four passenger trains a day, and passenger service ended the next year. The milk train was discontinued around 1958. Then, following large losses combined with a strike, the railroad ceased all operations by the latter part of 1961 when freight service ended.

No train service was available for over two years and until the state purchased the western section of the Rutland. This section, from Burlington to Bennington, was leased to the Vermont Railway Corporation. The Vermont Railway now renders freight service only, with two trains daily through Wallingford and other communities on its right of way.

In 1961, the railroad station at South Wallingford was taken apart and moved to Pawlet where it was reassembled and used as a coffee house and restaurant. The station at Wallingford was acquired by Fire District No. 1, and used to house the fire engines and serve as a meeting place for volunteer firemen. The station at East Wallingford was converted to a family residence.

*   *   *   *

Most people had less leisure time than they do today. At first, men in the fork factories worked six days a week from 7 in the morning until 6 at night. By 1912 working hours were from 7 to 5. Then considerably later on the work week was reduced to 5½ days, with Saturday afternoons off.

People also did different things with their leisure time. Then they had no television, and no radio until the 1920's. Popular sports were sliding and skating, baseball and swimming.

Ideal places for sliding were Sabe's Hill in Wallingford and the Dugway in South Wallingford. There was little traffic on either of these roads, especially at night, and sliding was permitted. At the steepest part of these roads there were water bars. When a sled hit them going at a good rate of speed, it took off for an instant like an airplane. Sliding on these hill roads after the snow became packed down was too fast and dangerous for small children, and so they used a short street or found a good hill in a nearby field or vacant lot.

One of the most popular sleds was the "flexible flyer" which was the easiest to steer. There were also "travesses" on which 5 or 6 people could ride, sitting one behind the other. The travesses were made by mounting a long board on two sleds. The front sled was on a swivel, and was steered by a rope fastened to each runner. The steerer braced his feet on a crossbar on the front of the long board.

Other winter sports of the sliding variety were called skiing and "jack jumping." The skiing had no more than a faint resemblance to present day skiing. For the small children, the skis were barrel staves with a toe strap in the middle made of a piece of leather or rubber. For the young folks, the skis were a long narrow board, turned up at the end and with a toe strap near the middle. Many were homemade. The ski slopes were any nearby hill in an open field. No technique was required. If you were real good, you made it all the way down the hill standing up. The smaller children had fun "jack jumping." The jack jumper was a barrel stave with a T-shaped seat attached to the middle. It was quite a trick to sit on that and slide for more than a few seconds.

With all the ponds around town there were plenty of places to skate, for example Fox Pond and Little Pond (out Elm Street Extension) in Wallingford. The skates were either strapped on or clamped on one's shoes with a skate key. No one had shoe skates. Sometimes in the evening a group would have a skating party, after clearing snow off the ice and building a bonfire to keep warm by.

In 1903, there was a basketball team that played teams from nearby towns. They practiced and played in Odd Fellows' Hall, with chicken-wire over the lights. Team members were James Cox, E. D. Cox, John Andre, John Senif, Charles Senif, Lew Sterling, and Robert Hebert.

There were two or three baseball teams during the "old days." William Roberts, who now lives in Springfield, Vermont, tells about one of these. "In the year 1913 there were no outdoor sports for young men in Wallingford. A group of us organized a baseball team, which we called the Wallingford Cubs, and played surrounding town teams. Our local field was the True Temper lot, which they let us use. It was not very smooth or level. We were very grateful to have it to play on. . . . We won a majority of our games."

The same field used by the town teams, where the Gulf station is now, was used for high school games until 1929 when Batcheller Field became available. People could sit on the top of the cliff on the east side of Route 7, much narrower then, and have a grandstand seat for the games.

In the 1870's, according to Birney Batcheller, the best swimming hole in town was in Otter Creek, but that was destroyed when the covered bridge was built. After that, and especially by 1919 when the Park Association was formed, Elfin Lake was the best place.

There were several tennis courts around town. One of the earliest, about 1910, was in back of the Library. Some years later, Father Griffin had a tennis court which was much in use.

Wallingford Cubs of 1913. L. to R., back row: William Roberts, Mgr. and 1st base; Paul Regimbald, 3d base. Wayne Hager, right field; Hennie Pickett, 2d base; Harry King, shortstop; John Preedom, center field; Bert Hebert, left field. Front row: Frank Hebert, pitcher; Roy LaFrancis, catcher.

In the evenings, going to the movies and to dances were favorite pastimes. Programs of illustrated slides became popular about 1910, and were accompanied by the singing of Mrs. Seeber. Soon after this, silent movies were shown in the Town Hall and were accompanied by piano playing. At first the music was improvised by the one who was playing, but soon the movie producers furnished a special score for each movie. Victor Lindsay is said to have been the first to provide this musical accompaniment. Others were Guy Savery, Lynn Seeber, Lowell Guerin, Bernard Fiske and Norris Fiske.

Around 1915, Guy Savery formed an orchestra which played for dances at the Town Hall or the Odd Fellows' Hall, and at nearby towns —Pawlet, Middletown, Tinmouth, Dorset, Danby. His orchestra also played at local events, including the 1917 high school graduation. Members of the orchestra were Guy Savery, piano; Guy Parker (from Middletown), violin; Harry Brown, drums; and Walter O'Brien, clarinet.

Much later, 1930-31, a group of high school students had a dance band for a short time. Members were Eunice Bugbee, piano; Norris Fiske and Philip Taft, violin; Paul Taft, saxophone; John Miller, drums. They played at dances in East Wallingford and South Wallingford, and were billed as "Doc Miller and his Pink Pills."

Many a good time was had when neighbors and friends gathered to square dance in the Jim Patch barn in Hartsboro. Local musicians took their turn on piano and fiddle.

In the early 20's, Asa (Ace) Ackley, a carpenter by trade, taught music to students in Wallingford, Danby, Tinmouth, and Middletown. He could play almost any instrument used in a band or orchestra except piano and slide trombone. Lessons were given at the local fire station. Once a year he brought all his students together to form an orchestra of some 25 to 30 pieces and gave a concert.

Radio was just starting to come in about this time. Neil Ward had the first set in the village, and he invited visitors to take turns listening with earphones. There was no speaker.

At various times, there has been a town band, and band concerts on summer evenings were popular and well attended. John Jones and George Fiske are names associated with the bands. East Wallingford had a cornet band which participated in the 1911 pageant.

People in the old days worked hard, and had few of the conveniences and amenities that we take for granted and even consider essential. Some years ago, a young girl asked her grandmother how she ever got along without wax paper, and zippers, and electricity, and things like that. "Well," the grandmother replied, "I don't know, but we thought we got along fine."

Chapter 3

Town Government

ORGANIZATION

The following quotation is from the *Inventory of Town, Village, and City Archives of Vermont*, Volume XXV.

"Organization of the town government was effected in 1778 under the Vermont Constitution of 1777 but before laws had been enacted on town officers and their duties. The settlers followed the procedure of Connecticut, from which most of them came. With the exception that the officers usually designated as selectmen were called simply 'the Committee,' the organization followed the lines afterward adopted for Vermont towns."

The officers who now are elected at the March town meeting are Moderator, Clerk, Treasurer, First and Second Constable, Grand Juror, Town Agent, Tax Collector, Selectmen, Listers, Auditors, and Trustees of Public Money. Then at the general elections in November, a Representative to the State Legislature and Justices of the Peace are elected.

All other officers are appointed by the Selectmen, except the Health Officer, who is nominated by the Selectmen and appointed for a four-year term by the State Health Commissioner. Appointed officers include Assistant Clerk, Assistant Treasurer, Assistant Health Officer, Town Service Officer, Tree Warden, Pound Keeper, Weigher of Coal, Fire Warden, Deputy Fire Warden, 3 Fence Viewers, Planning Commission members and Administrative Officer, Board of Adjustment members, and Representative to the Regional Planning Commission. One of the Selectmen is usually appointed Road Commissioner.

The Selectmen, Justices of the Peace, and Town Clerk make up the Board of Civil Authority; the Selectmen and Health Officers make up the Town Board of Health.

The duties of the officers are generally what their titles would indicate. However, some explanation for the Town Service Officer, the Fence Viewer, and a note about the Pound Keeper, may be of interest. The Town Service Officer serves as "on the spot" representative of the Department of Social Welfare. He is directly responsible to district officers who are in charge of general assistance programs, and who also administer orientation and training sessions. He helps applicants apply for aid and authorizes payment for emergency medical services.

The Fence Viewers are to examine the fences within the town upon request. When requested to act, the Fence Viewers will make a division of fence, or appraise the value of a fence made or repaired, or determine the sufficiency of a fence.

Until the middle 1930's, there were usually three Pound Keepers, one in each village. Now there is only one for the town.

Although a Pound Keeper may be needed, his duties are light compared with what they used to be. For example, back in 1906 when Charles D. Seward was Pound Keeper, not all farmers mended their fences and their cattle would get out and into the gardens and crops of nearby farmers. These farmers naturally would complain to the Pound Keeper and insist that he take prompt action. The necessary prompt action was to drive the cattle to his own farm, which was the Town Pound. This was never easy and sometimes quite difficult; the law stated that if the cattle were driven by their home farmland they would have to be delivered to their owner's barnyard and could not be impounded, so it was necessary to drive them in a round about way that would not pass the offending farmer's property. Once the cattle were in the Pound Keeper's Pound, he was able to extract payment for damages and obtain assurances from the farmer the he would mend his fences and keep his cattle from invading his neighbor's property.

SELECTMEN

The Selectmen are the governing body of the township; in accord with Vermont law, every township annually elects one Selectman for three years, on a staggered basis. Each township must have 3 Selectmen. The Selectmen fill any vacancies on the Board between elections by appointment. Each town may vote for two additional Selectmen for one year terms, and may vote to have a Town Manager.

Wallingford in 1975 has five selectmen and no town manager. Duties and actions of the selectmen are financed through town tax monies (general fund), federal forest money, and state gasoline tax money for road construction. At different times there are special funds, such as the "flood repair" money in 1973, now "Federal Sharing Funds," and from time to time federal grants. These funds must pay for all town government expenses except those for schools and fire districts.

A major responsibility of the selectmen is the repair and maintenance of town roads and bridges, the laying out of new roads, and the "throwing up" of those of limited use and too costly to maintain. The selectmen deal with complaints of all kinds—concerning abandoned buildings, vandalism, noise, dog bites, health hazards, and damage caused by water, trees, and soil erosion. They prepare and enact needed town ordinances. They are responsible for the care and repair of town-owned buildings and equipment, streets, and sidewalks, and they are directly or indirectly concerned with town financing, planning and development, and with the protection, health, and well-being of the community.

THE FREEMAN'S OATH

Age and residence requirements for becoming a legal voter of the town of Wallingford have been relaxed in recent years. However, all new voters still must take this Freeman's Oath: "You solemnly swear (or affirm) that whenever you give your vote or suffrage, touching any matter that concerns the State of Vermont, you will do it so as in your conscience you shall judge will most conduce to the best good of the same, as established by the Constitution, without fear or favor of any person." Vermont Constitution, Chapter 2, Section 34.

TOWN MANAGER

At a special Town Meeting on November 3, 1961, it was voted to have a Town Manager. The Vote was Yes 107, No 95, Blank 1. In December 1961, T. R. Nutting was hired as the first Town Manager. He was followed by James Lowe from 1964 to 1966, by William Parker from 1966 to 1968, by Dean Brown from 1968 to 1969, and by John Risher from 1969 to 1971. Then at Town Meeting in March 1971, it was voted not to hire any more Town Managers, the vote being 202 not to hire, 172 in favor of hiring, and 60 not voting.

PLANNING and ZONING

Planning had a hard time getting established. The first Commission lasted only one year (1966), the second, two years (1967-68). There were reasons for this; there wasn't much professional help available then, also there couldn't have been much incentive because many people in town didn't want Zoning anyway; they were of a mind that anyone could do whatever he wanted with his own property regardless of the effect on his neighbor or the community. Then in 1969, at a meeting in the Town Hall, a vocal minority vigorously promoted Zoning to protect the Town from an anticipated invasion of mobile homes, and mobile home parks such as those established in neighboring towns. Also by 1969 needed guidance and professional help were available from the Rutland Regional Planning Commission. So in that year Interim Zoning was adopted and a new Planning Commission was appointed by the Selectmen.

To provide temporary regulation of development while Zoning Regulations were being prepared, the Selectmen on July 31, 1969, adopted Interim Zoning for a two year period. A year later, however, a decision not to grant a variance was appealed by the person concerned to the Rutland County Court and the Court declared the Interim Zoning

CITIZEN SMITH   By Dave Gerard

"Poor Hoadley! He accepted an appointment to the zoning and planning board!"

Reprinted by permission of Dave Gerard and The Register and Tribune Syndicate

invalid, on a technicality, because notice of the required public hearing on the regulation was published only 13 days in advance, and not 15 days as required by law. Then on July 31, 1970, Interim Regulations were again adopted by the Selectmen and remained in effect until March 1971, when they were replaced by more comprehensive regulations.

The members of the Planning Commission appointed in 1969 were Francis Hoadley, Laszlo Kerr, Julian Klock, Paul Mooney, Frank Morrell, Roland Seward, Frank Stafford and Frederick Thurlow. This Commission produced a Development plan, Zoning Regulations, and Subdivision Regulations.

The Development Plan was adopted by the Selectmen in October, 1970. The proposed Zoning Regulations were approved by the voters of the Town on March 1971, by a narrow margin, 213 to 211. Obviously many townspeople did not want zoning and in December of that year the legality of both the Plan and the Zoning Regulation was challenged; but in February, in a court test, the Rutland County Court declared that the Plan was valid and the Zoning Regulations valid and enforceable. Then in March 1972, the voters were asked whether they wished to continue Zoning and this time they approved it by a margin of 33 votes, 196 to 163. However, it was not until the Regulations were made more flexible, in the light of experience in administering them, that they became generally acceptable. These amended regulations were approved by those voting at a special Town Meeting on September 1972 by a vote of 231 to 90. The Development Plan (1970) was also amended and this amended Plan was adopted by the Selectmen in February 1973.

The proposed Subdivision Regulations were approved, the first time around, in March 1973, the vote being 253 to 116.

The Administrative Officer must administer the Zoning and Subdivision Regulations literally and may grant permits only when the proposed development is in conformance with the Regulations.

The Administrative Officer is appointed for a three year term by the Planning Commission with the approval of the Selectmen. This position was first held by Town Manager John Risher until he resigned in 1970. Then William Wedwaldt was Administrative Officer in 1971, Robert Crosby in 1972, Lyman Cousens in 1973, and Jay Johnstone in 1975.

Any interested person may appeal to the Board of Adjustment any decision or action taken by the Administrative officer. The Board may grant or reject the appeal; but it may grant a variance from the Regulations only if all the conditions specified in the Vermont Planning and Development Act are met.

Members of the Board of Adjustment are appointed, and terms of office determined, by the Selectmen. Members of the first Board, appointed in 1971, were Clarence Barlow, Jr., Inez Dawson, Laszlo Kerr, Carolyn Patch, and Frank Stafford.

CARE OF THE POOR

One of the great changes that have occurred over the years is in the care of the poor. In the beginning, care of the poor was auctioned off at town meeting, and they were placed in the homes of the lowest bidders. This arrangement was discontinued in 1840 when the first poor farm was purchased. Town reports during the decade 1910–19 gave the names and ages of persons at the farm and concluded with a statement that all were well provided for and properly clothed. Then in 1921 the report stated: "In regard to the town farm, your auditors would say. That while there is nothing seriously wrong there with either the farm or the dairy management, the cows and stables are not what they should be. There being but one guest there at the present time there may be some question as to what the town should do with the farm. Some say sell it—others, rent it to some family and hire them to take care of the poor; while others say, make the necessary repairs and continue as we have been doing."

The town bought and sold a number of poor farms; the last one was sold in 1951. By this time direct payments were being made to, or on behalf of, persons in need, with reimbursements from the State for part of the cost.

Although the State of Vermont assumed all welfare responsibilities in 1968, the town's welfare obligations did not end until 1970 when all the remaining hospital bills were paid. In 1972 the legislature abolished the office of Overseer of the Poor and placed general assistance to the poor and transients within the Department of Social Welfare. A town Service officer, whose duties have been previously described, acts under the direction of the Commissioner of Social Welfare.

SCHOOLS

During the early years, the town was divided into school districts which were largely self-governing. The number of districts and their boundaries changed often, as the number of scholars in the neighborhoods changed. In 1892 the Legislature abolished the multiple district system, and all schools in the town were brought under the direction of town school directors.

The annual school meeting is held on town meeting day, after the town meeting, and voting is by separate ballot in the same polls. A budget is voted on, and one or more school directors elected. Since 1895, the usual number of directors has been three, except for the years 1971 to 1974, when there were five; they serve for staggered three-year terms. Wallingford also elects three of the seven directors for Union School District No. 40, which operates Mill River Union High School for junior and senior high school students from Clarendon, Shrewsbury, and Wallingford.

ELECTED OFFICERS 1910-1975
MODERATOR – TOWN CLERK – SELECTMEN
TOWN REPRESENTATIVE

MODERATOR

A. G. Stone
S. C. Saunders
Rev. A. C. Griffin
George Kelley
C. N. Foote
Ralph R. Dana
John P. Hoadley
Leland W. Lawson
Roland Q. Seward

TOWN CLERK

W. P. Cary
Winifred Saunders
C. N. Foote
Bertha Savery
Mildred O. Lindstone
Arlene M. Doty

SELECTMEN

Hiram J. Fales
William Stone
Arthur B. Seward
Eugene Smith
Maurice R. Hawkins
William F. Hager
Myron H. Roberts
John C. Doty
E. J. Chilson
A. W. Duval
George H. Stafford
Edmund N. Edgerton
Roy H. Stafford
Charles R. Cole
George E. Eldred
Donald Leach
Forest E. Graves
Charles N. Foote
Arthur B. Davison
Ralph E. Stafford
Allyn B. Seward
Bert A. McClure
Herbert Underwood
Leo G. Benjamin
Albert H. Kelley
Albert Perry, Sr.
Ralph Lidstone
Stephen Maranville
C. Edgar Stevens
Harold Underwood
Sherwin W. Fish
Lowell Seward
Donald S. Parker
James Davenport, Jr.
Hugh Young
Richard Kendall

SELECTMEN (Cont'd.)

Gerald Stack
Edward Patch
Jack Schippers
Francis R. Parker
Frank Bruce
William Parker
Leland Lawson
James Kennedy
Donald J. Parker
Carolyn Patch
James Marquis

TOWN REPRESENTATIVE

D. W. Stafford
Addison G. Stone
G. L. Batcheller
H. G. Savery
H. D. Hopkins
A. R. Seward
Christopher Stafford
Rev. O. R. Houghton
Ella B. Seward
C. J. Waters
B. C. Batcheller
George W. Kelley
Roy A. Hatch
Charles N. Foote
Robert W. Hopkins
Guy L. Stafford
Ralph R. Dana
Edmund Edgerton
Farand A. Dean
Bert A. McClure
Bertha Savery
John P. Hoadley
Ralph E. Stafford*

*Ralph Stafford has served in the Vermont Legislature as Representative or Senator for 24 years.

WALLINGFORD FIRE DISTRICT NO. 1

Fire District No. 1 includes most of the village of Wallingford. It was incorporated in 1906 by a special act of the legislature, which gave it authority to provide for fire protection and street lighting, and to make contracts for water.

The first Fire District meeting was held on June 15, 1907. Members of the three-man governing body, called the Prudential Committee, were H. B. Barden, Chairman, and Charles Batcheller and Caleb Paris, Committeemen. Also elected by the voters of the district were A. C. Blanchard, Clerk, W. P. Cary, Treasurer, Robert Hopkins, Tax Collector, C. V. Howley, Fire Chief, and Elwin Burdett, Assistant Fire Chief.

The primary inventory was a thousand feet of 2 1/2" hose and two hose carts. By 1910 the operating budget of the District had grown to more than $4000, with funding obtained through property taxation.

Power for street lighting was obtained from the Rutland Railway Light and Power Company.

The Fire District maintained a contract with the Wallingford Water Company, a privately owned company, for rental of fire hydrants and use of water for fire fighting when required. In 1907 the Water Company had built a small reservoir east of the village, adjacent to Roaring Brook, and constructed a distribution system in the village. Water was fed to the reservoir by gravity from springs located in the natural watershed of the brook.

An amendment to the Fire District charter in 1929 gave it the right to borrow money and to sell bonds. Later that year, $50,000 of debenture bonds were sold and all the property, water rights, equipment, and water system of the Water Company were acquired by the District. Soon after this purchase the important springs were rebuilt and improvements were made in the distribution system. The District set up a separate department for water, with income supported by water rents. A total of 46 people worked on the water system in its first year of operation by the Fire District, and the expenditures were over $10,000. This sum was not exceeded until 1944 when a new reservoir was constructed adjacent to the one built by the former Water Company.

In the early days of the Fire District an alarm was given by tolling bells. The District was apparently divided into four subdistricts, but where the lines were drawn is not known. The bell at the Congregational Church sounded the alarm for subdistrict 1, the bell at the Baptist Church for subdistrict 2, and a bell at the American Fork and Hoe Company for subdistrict 4. It is not known what was sounded for a fire in subdistrict 3.

Small fires were common, and were usually put out before any serious damage occurred. Then in March 1924 there were several major

Wallingford village, North Main Street area, by Donald Wickenmayer

fires. Fire destroyed the finishing shop of the American Fork and Hoe Company. The fire company was called out twice more that week, to a fire in Townsend's Garage (estimated loss $1000) and on Saturday night when Royal Thayer's sugar house burned down. Word of its destruction spread in the village and was announced from the pulpit on Sunday morning. That afternoon a group of volunteers rebuilt it and sugaring operations were resumed, no sap having been lost.

In 1937 the Fire District replaced its Model T hose-carrying truck with a 500-gallon-per-minute pumper mounted on a 1936 Ford truck. But the department still lacked enough hose in good condition to cope with major fires which occurred in 1938. One of these burned the A. W. Newton barn. Water was pumped from Otter Creek about 1000 feet away. The hose were in poor condition and a number burst, but with the aid of the Rutland Fire Department the house and garage were saved. Another large fire that year was at the Wallingford Baking Company. Damage there was estimated at $8000. Water from the hydrants lasted only a short time. Water was pumped from Roaring Brook and a truckload of additional hose was obtained from the American Fork and Hoe Company. This enabled the firemen to save the houses nearby.

As the Department needed additional money during the late 1930's, Albert Bersaw and his committee raised it by holding dances at the East Wallingford Masonic Hall and by bingo and card parties. With the money thus obtained they bought rubber coats and boots, and converted a part of the fire station into a meeting room.

In 1945 the American Fork and Hoe Company deeded two large parcels of land to the District. One of these is located at the southern end of Elfin Lake and known as the Boys' Camp. The property included a main lodge building, an infirmary, and a number of small cabins.

The Camp was operated in the summer months, by lease or rental. During the 1940's and 1950's, the camp was used by church and 4H groups for one- and two-week camps for local youngsters. The Shawnee Institute from Pennsylvania had sessions of its international camp there, under the direction of Rev. Carl Voss of Rutland. But the small income from these non-profit organizations often did not cover the cost of regular maintenance and of vandalism. So now the property is under long lease to the Rutland Mental Health Service. A well was drilled and a mobile home installed to provide a year-round residence for the superintendent. The camp has been named Kritter Kamp.

The other parcel of land given by the American Fork and Hoe Company lies between the railroad and Otter Creek and is known as Stone Meadow. It has been considered a promising source of additional water. Development of a new source of water adequate for future needs has been postponed in part because of the expense required. An engineering study indicated that adequate water for immediate needs could be provided by stopping leaks in the present distribution system and a number have been found and repaired.

Public water systems now must meet Vermont State standards. Accordingly, the water is chlorinated and test samples analysed to assure meeting the standards. Recently 6″ diameter mains were installed on Deerfield Drive and Elm Street.

POLLUTION CONTROL PROJECT

The Vermont Legislature passed a law in 1960 which enabled the Department of Water Resources to set standards of quality for all bodies of water in the state. Otter Creek failed to meet the standards because of the dumping of raw sewerage from nearby communities, including Wallingford. Consequently Wallingford was directed to submit suitable plans for sewerage disposal. This was to be done by October, 1962.

At a special Town hearing on May 8, 1962, all those present decided that it would be the responsibility of each individual and business to comply. Many home owners installed new septic tanks. However, at several homes and commercial buildings satisfactory disposal systems could not be installed because of insufficient land around the building, unfavorable soil conditions, or because they were too close to the creek.

In 1963, Governor Philip H. Hoff issued an executive order requiring strict and expeditious enforcement of the statutes concerning pollution of waters, and Wallingford was directed to comply. Some sort of sewerage system had to be built. However, the cost of constructing a sewerage system and treatment plant was so great that the Fire District could not undertake it without financial aid from Federal and State agencies. Little was done until late in 1966, when Wallingford was notified that it had until June 1, 1967 to submit a plan for pollution abatement. The Town Manager, William Parker, working with state engineers, then filed an application with the State of Vermont for preliminary planning funds. A sum of $6500 was approved by the Fire District, and the Dufresne-Henry Engineering Corp. of Springfield, Vt. was hired to make the study. Upon completion of this preliminary study an application was made for advance planning funds, $24,000 was approved, and Dufresne-Henry began work on the final plans.

At a special meeting of the Fire District held on March 9, 1971, authorization was given for $175,000 as the District's share for the construction of a Sewerage Collection and Treatment Facility. The vote was 115 in favor and 59 opposed. An option to purchase land for the sewerage treatment facility was obtained on the so-called "Island," a

View of Sewage Disposal Plant

small parcel of land surrounded by Otter Creek and the old canal used by the Fork and Hoe factory. A right-of-way was given by the True Temper Corporation.

The Prudential Committee appointed William Parker as "Authorized Representative" to administer and supervise the project. Contracts were awarded to Waggaman and Collyer Construction Co. of Glens Falls, N. Y., and Arthur Whitcomb Construction Co. of Keene, N. H. Work began in April, 1972, and the project was completed and in operation in June, 1973.

The total cost of the project, including construction, legal fees, rights-of-way, surveying, engineering, and planning, was $720,000. Grants totalling $545,000 were received from the State of Vermont, Federal Environmental Protective Agency (EPA), and the Farmers Home Administration (FHA).

The Wallingford Sewerage Collection and Treatment Facility was well built and has operated successfully. As of June, 1975, there were 160 homes, plus commercial and industrial buildings, connected to this facility.

RURAL VOLUNTEER HOSE COMPANY

The Rural Volunteer Hose Company was organized in 1955 to give fire protection to Wallingford residents outside the village limits. It serves the Otter Creek valley from the Clarendon line to the Danby line, and has mutual aid agreements with surrounding towns.

Equipment of the Hose Company consists of a truck with a 1000 gallon tank, two portable pumps, and small fire-fighting tools. The Company pays its share of Fire District No. 1 expenses for the fire station and for firemen's insurance.

The thirty volunteer firemen in District No. 1, also serve with the Rural Volunteer Hose Company. All firemen are required to complete a 45-hour fire school conducted by a Vermont state certified fire instructor. They hold monthly meetings at the fire station on the second Tuesday of each month.

The District has one 500-gallon-per-minute front-line pumper and a utility truck to carry fire-fighting equipment. The alarm system is connected to the phones of ten different firemen, and when the FIRE number is dialed, the phone rings at all ten homes. The alarm can be activated from each of these home phones and also from the fire station.

Responsibilities of Fire District No. 1 have increased considerably since its inception in 1907. Now included are fire protection, street lighting, sidewalk plowing, maintenance of water and sewer systems, the Kritter Kamp, and the "Stone Meadow" property.

MEMBERS OF PRUDENTIAL COMMITTEE 1910-1975
Fire District No. 1

H. B. Barden	R. W. Congdon	Edward Patch
E. L. Senif	Francis Hoadley	Clois Brown
W. C. Mason	Arthur Vivian	Fred Thurlow
F. H. Hoadley	Carl Eastman	Ola Weatherby
A. W. Andrews	Waldo White	Earl Patch
W. A. Davis	Kenneth Fish	David Kelley
W. F. Hager	Fred Capell	Michael Brown
A. W. Ferguson	Donald Mead	J. Robert Stewart
J. P. Hoadley	James Ingalls	Clovis Leach
C. V. Howley	Clyde Patch	Walter Wade
C. N. Foote		

W. A. Davis served consecutively for 38 years.

Hoadleys—F. H., J. P., and Francis—served consecutively for 46 years.

EAST WALLINGFORD FIRE DISTRICT NO. 2

Fire District No. 2 was organized in September, 1947, and then covered one square mile. Members of the Prudential Committee, the governing body, were Clarence L'Hommedieu, Harold Pelkey, and Allyn Seward. The Fire Chief was Clarence L'Hommedieu; Clerk, Mary L'Hommedieu; Treasurer, Lewis Bumps; Tax Collector, Ralph Dana; Auditors, Emma Bumps and Nancy Graves.

The first equipment was a portable pump and 1000 feet of 1½" hose, which was carried on a trailer built by the firemen. There were 15 volunteer firemen. A firetruck was bought in the fall of 1955, and a firehouse completed in February, 1956. It was built almost entirely by volunteer labor, on land purchased from Ralph Dana.

In 1971, most of the property above the Gulf was added to the district, thus more than doubling its original size. Poll taxes and personal property taxes have now been dropped, and revenues are obtained from a tax on buildings only.

All 15 volunteer firemen complete a fire school course conducted by a Vermont State certified instructor.

Members of Prudential Committee, 1947-1975

Clarence L'Hommedieu	Leo Benjamin
Harold Pelkey	Edward Dana
Allyn Seward	Robert Nash
Alvin Belcher	John Maranville
Edson Merrill	Stanley Seward

Alvin Belcher served as Fire Chief from 1953 until his death in 1975.

Chapter 4
Business and Industry I

The first industries in the town developed to meet the immediate needs of the settlers, and most of them located along streams to make use of water power. There were blacksmith shops, saw mills, tanneries, grist mills to grind the grain, and fulling mills to prepare the woolen cloth made at home for sewing—to scour out the grease, dye and press it. By 1820 there were in the township, as listed in Thompson's *Gazetteer*, two grist mills, ten saw mills, two fulling mills, two carding machines, one cotton factory, five stores, one tavern, two distilleries, one furnace, four tanneries, and six blacksmiths. The locations of these enterprises were not given so they cannot be surely identified, but histories of the times describe such industries. The available information about some of them can be summed up very briefly; others become important in the economic life of the town and had a long history.

In Wallingford village, there was a cluster of mills—a grist mill, a saw mill, and a fulling mill—near Otter Creek on what is now Elm Street. They all got their power from a dam built in 1788 by Asahel and Jedediah Jackson. A forge had been built near the dam, and Alexander Miller also had a blacksmith shop where the Stone Shop now stands, built in the early 1800's. His tannery was across the street. There was another tannery on the Dyer Townsend farm south of the village, and one over east near Mill River, built in 1815 by Mathial Smead and operated for more than 50 years by a succession of owners.

In South Wallingford in 1795, Stutely Stafford bought from John Reed a saw and grist mill on the east side of Otter Creek, and his sons operated it. Later the building was used by W. W. Kelley as a marble finishing mill, and it finally burned in 1905. Jonas Wood built a cotton factory in 1815, also near the Creek, and this building burned in 1830. A forge was built and operated for some years on the site. It was followed in 1864 by a mill building used first for finishing marble, then, in the 1880's for a pulp mill.

MINING IN SOUTH WALLINGFORD

The furnace mentioned in the *Gazetteer* was probably near the iron ore deposit east of South Wallingford village, on the banks of Homer Stone Brook. It was worked for a time starting in 1815, and again about 1880 when Andrew Carnegie acquired it and built a railroad spur to the location. However, the ore contained a high percentage of manganese and iron made from it was hard and brittle.

On the other side of the brook is a deposit of kaolin or porcelain clay which was mined for a time. Graphite has also been found in South Wallingford.

BATCHELLER AND SONS COMPANY

In 1835, Lyman Batcheller of Arlington bought a blacksmith and triphammer shop on Main Street, together with water rights, for the manufacture of pitch forks. This was the shop which Alexander Miller had owned thirty years before. The factory burned in 1848 and the Stone Shop was erected on the site, with townspeople contributing labor and money for the new building. Additions were made to the building, and the forks were polished in a building across the road where the water was used again for power as it flowed, partly underground, to the creek. By 1865 more space and power were needed, so Batcheller and Sons purchased the property by the Otter Creek dam. The existing saw mill and a shoe-peg factory on the site of the old forge were both adapted to their needs, and a warehouse built. A forge and triphammer shop was constructed beside the dam, where a grist mill and later a tanbark mill had stood. In 1882 the firm was incorporated as Batcheller and Sons Company, although Lyman Batcheller, Sr., had died some years before.

Farther north on Otter Creek was another factory site and water privilege. Franklin Post built a factory there in 1869 and manufactured pitchforks in competition with the Batchellers, but only for a few years. The building stood empty for a time, then was taken over by H. C. Cole and John D. Miller, who made ox-bows there.

OX-BOWS

An old newspaper account was found of an interview with Byron Leonard, who worked on the bows. They were usually made, he said, of sweet or bitter walnut; for the cheapest bows, red elm might be used. The same crew of men worked in the woods cutting and splitting the logs, and then in the mill doing the shaping and finishing operations. Occasionally an order was received from Africa or India for bows to be used on a team of elephants. These big bows, heavy and hard to handle, were always made of sweet walnut wood for strength.

WALLINGFORD MANUFACTURING COMPANY

The North Shop building was again used for the manufacture of agricultural tools when H. B. Barden and his brother moved their small tool business from Granville, New York to Wallingford. The business was incorporated in 1902 as the Wallingford Manufacturing Company, and expanded its line to include all kinds of hand tools for farm and garden. In 1910 it was taken over by a Canadian concern, the Welland

Vale Manufacturing Company, Ltd.   The building was enlarged and modernized, and A. W. Ferguson of Willoughby, Ohio, was installed as manager.

AMERICAN FORK & HOE COMPANY

In 1902, Batcheller & Sons Company became the Batcheller Works of the American Fork & Hoe Company. This new company was formed when a number of small tool businesses, some of them family businesses like the Batchellers', merged and established headquarters in Cleveland, Ohio. William C. Mason, who had been associated with the Batchellers for some years, was the local manager. In 1911, he was in poor health and R. C. Taft, a young engineer, was sent from Cleveland to be acting manager. Mr. Mason's health did not improve, he resigned and moved with his family to California, and Mr. Taft became manager. Charles Batcheller, a grandson of Lyman Batcheller, was the only member of that family still connected with the business. He operated one of the triphammers and was proud of his skill. He went out of his way to assure Mr. Taft that he wanted no special treatment because of his name.

The Batchellers from the first had made quality tools which were in demand locally, in the rest of the country, and abroad. Other tools had been added to the line after the move to larger quarters; an 1870 price list shows several kinds of forks, hoes, and rakes. The triphammer shop was enlarged from time to time, and a steam engine installed to give extra power when the creek ran low. It is said that an attempt was made to turn water from Fox Pond into Otter Creek at times of low water by digging a ditch between them, but that it failed because the level of Fox Pond is lower than that of the creek.

At this time (1912) the tools were still being made about as they had been since the early years of the business. Blanks for the forks were cut from steel bars in a pattern that used the steel without waste, each cut piece meshing with the next as in a jig-saw puzzle. The tines and shank were formed under a triphammer, bent to shape on a device called a headbender, then tempered by being heated once more and quenched in oil. The forks were polished by tumbling them with water and gravel in large cylinders. The Stone Shop had been put back into use for this operation, and the sound of the cylinders turning was heard on South Main Street until the 1920's. Assembling, finishing, and packing the tools was done in the tall gray finishing shop on Elm Street; handles were of white ash, as always.

About 1914, a rolling operation using steel dies for drawing the fork tines began to replace the triphammers, although the older men in the shop were sure the forks would not be as well made by the new process. The wet tumble finish lasted longer; it was replaced between 1937 and

1940 by a process which involved polishing each tine on an emery belt. And by this time the trade mark was being branded into the handle instead of being carried on a printed, pasted-on label.

In March of 1924, the finishing shop burned. After a time it was replaced by a smaller masonry building, used for tumbling and polishing the forks because it still had water power. The building is now the Vermont Tubbs plant. Later that same year the company acquired the property of the Wallingford Manufacturing Company. The deed listed 17 parcels, among them the factory that Franklin Post had built in 1869 with its ten acres of land, "the use of the water and the use of the ditch or canal therefore," and several houses in the area near the factory.

In the very early years, there had been competition, even some bad feeling between the two companies, but after 1900 there seems to have been more a spirit of friendly rivalry, especially after both shops became parts of larger organizations and sales were managed from company headquarters. The north shop was somewhat larger, employing between 125 and 200 men during those years, but both made similar items and their best quality, the True Temper and Wallingford brands, were comparable. Now, in 1924, the north shop and the south shop were merged,

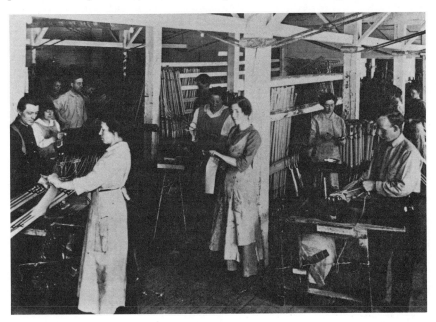

Paint Room, Wallingford Manufacturing Company. L. to R., Fred LaBarge, Vina Hebert, Mary Macfarlane, George Reynolds, Eva Senif, Nellie Seeber, Harold Eastman, Marie Parker, Lucia Buswell, Susie Seeber, Lynn Seeber, Mrs. Earl, Mrs. G. Madden.

with Mr. Taft as manager. Mr. Ferguson, who had a background in business and banking, went to Cleveland as treasurer of the American Fork and Hoe Company.

The 1920's were a period of change as well as expansion for the combined tool company. The market for agricultural implements was changing as agriculture changed, from many small family farms to fewer and larger ones. The officers also became aware of the recreation market when idle farms began to be bought by "summer people," and when a company engineer at another plant developed a process for tapering steel tubing so it could be used for fishing rods and golf club shafts. The first local move into this recreation market was in 1921, when land that the company owned on the west side of Elfin Lake was divided into lots for cottages and the lots were put up for sale. Then in 1926, the Old Stone Shop was remodelled for a tearoom, the hotel was purchased, and, in 1927, land was acquired at the south end of Elfin Lake for a boy's camp.

THE OLD STONE SHOP

The Company's architect from Cleveland was in charge of renovating the Old Stone Shop and changing it from fork factory to Tea Room. Great care was taken to alter it no more than necessary. The two fireplaces are of stone to harmonize with the stone walls, which were left uncovered and are pleasing to the eye. The fireplace at the north end uses the original brick chimney that carried the smoke from Lyman Batcheller's forge. The flagstone floor covers the ditches where the polishing cylinders turned, as well as the part of the mill-race that was inside the building, where village boys sometimes caught trout. A part of the raceway can still be seen in the yard. Displayed on the east wall of the building is a collection of old farm tools, some from Lyman Batcheller's era, and samples of the blanks used to make forks and other tools. There is also a model of the rolling machine used for drawing the fork tines after the triphammers were no longer used.

The tearoom opened in the spring of 1927, and was operated by a Mr. and Mrs. Bennett from Massachusetts the first year. Then Lora Clark, whose late husband had run the hotel, managed it until her death in 1939. From then until it was closed by the war, Cornelia Tarbell managed the tearoom and Mrs. Louise Ritcher also had her Caravan Craft Shop in the building.

THE HOTEL

The purchase of the hotel in 1926 came about almost by chance. Property put on the market by the Wallingford Hotel Company consisted of three parcels, the hotel and its contents, certain rights in the "common," and about six acres of land known as the Ice Bed lot, its eastern boundary "a line on the mountain as far up as timber grows." The company's chief interest was in this third parcel of land; they planned to harvest the ash trees on it for handles, and to sell the other two parcels. However, because the recreation market was growing, and because of advertising and public relations possibilities, the hotel was not sold. Instead, the building was handsomely remodelled, under the direction of Carl Rowley, the company architect, and renamed True Temper Inn. The former billiard room was made into a display room for company products. L. G. Treadway of Williamstown, Mass., became managing director, and the Inn was one of his chain of Real New England Inns.

The "common," which was the vacant lot at the corner of Main and School Streets, and the Inn's sideyard, was also purchased. It had come into possession of the Baptist Church, and the members were deeply divided about selling to the company. By a close vote they finally decided to sell it, but to put restrictions in the deed about its use. "No buildings or structures of any kind or gas service pumps, portable peanut, popcorn or candy stands shall be erected or maintained on said premises. . . . Neither shall any cars be parked upon said land . . . all the property deeded shall be used exclusively for a lawn, park or common."

The hotel was old when the company bought it, having been started in 1824 from a design by John Ives. During its first century it had many owners and many names—"The First Temperance Hotel in the World," the "Tavern House," the "Wallingford Hotel," and had also housed stores and offices. In 1892 W. D. Hulett renovated it and enlarged it to 4 stories and 31 rooms, renaming it the "New Wallingford." A brochure of that time offered fine dining, with vegetables, milk, cream, and butter from their own farm. It assured prospective guests of a good livery, with all classes of vehicles, careful drivers, and saddle horses, as well as ample accommodations for guests bringing their own horses. Directions for reaching Wallingford by train were also given. Nearby attractions were listed, including the "Ice Cave at the foot of White Rock Mountain," and Elfin Lake and Otter Creek, where the hotel provided boating facilities. Excellent fishing was mentioned.

A good many summer visitors stopped at the hotel through the years, as well as salesmen or "drummers" between trains. An old account mentions salesmen's checker games with "Doc" Ainsworth. People from the community found the hotel convenient also—the barber shop, the bar, the billiard room (no one under 16 admitted), and the livery stable, which went out of business around 1914. Theodore Roosevelt spoke from the hotel's front porch on a swing through Vermont during the 1912 presidential campaign. His arrival was delayed, and Clifford

Cary is said to have taken advantage of the delay to amuse the crowd. He persuaded Harry Townsend to drive him, bowing, smiling, and waving in candidate style from an open car, coming slowly from South Main Street up to the hotel.

True Temper Inn opened in the spring of 1927, with Noble Miller as manager and a number of local people employed. For the next few summers it was quite a lively place, enjoyed by people from the area and summer visitors. E. G. Tileston and then Charles Danolds followed Mr. Miller as manager. For several years the company's annual meeting was held at the Inn in August, and this event brought the officers and directors and their families to Wallingford. "Cleveland office" came to mean people whom the community knew, and the company men seemed to take a special interest in the town where they had so many projects under way. At one time there was a suggestion that the company would be willing to paint all the houses in town white, if the residents chose to have it look more "New England," but nothing came of the suggestion.

THE BOYS' CAMP

The boys' camp project was planned to boost patronage at the Inn, since parents visiting their camper sons would be potential guests. The buildings were on the site of the Cary camp, the first cottage on Elfin Lake, at its south end. Its name, Kawawin, was coined from Indian words meaning True Temper. It was operated by Keewaydin Camps, an established group of camps in New England, for younger boys. A prospectus for the camp stated that "it is our intention to run the camp in a True Temper way, so that the boys will have minds keen-edged and tempered for the tasks of life."

TUBBS SNOW SHOES

In 1931, the company purchased the W. F. Tubbs Snow Shoe Company of Norway, Maine, and moved it to Wallingford. Those who planned the acquisition were looking for other products which would use the same materials and skills as garden tools, but be marketed at a different season and thus even out the work load in the shop. Also, the Tubbs Company made skis as well as snow shoes, and it was hoped that the dark heart-wood of the ash, not suitable for handles, could be used for children's skis, at that time usually stained dark anyway. However, this market did not develop as hoped, and few skis were made here.

The manufacture of snow shoes and snow shoe chairs became one of Wallingford's most interesting industries. Snow shoe frames are cut from straight-grain white ash wood, steamed and bent to shape, and laced with high quality rawhide. The lacing is done with wet rawhide which tightens as it dries. They are then dipped in spar varnish. Jack Burgess came from Maine with the Tubbs Company to train the Wallingford workers in the art of making snow shoes. Many Wallingford men and women became excellent "lacers."

Snowshoes and snowshoe chairs have been shipped all over the world. The old W. F. Tubbs Company made snowshoes and dog sleds for explorer Robert E. Peary's first two trips to the polar regions. The Wallingford company made snowshoes and chairs for Admiral Byrd's second trip to the South Pole. With continued interest in winter sports, more and more people have taken up snowshoeing. It is one of the least expensive sports, and requires no expensive lessons. If you can walk, you can snowshoe.

The depression of the 1930's naturally had its effect on local industry. The newly acquired snowshoe business added welcome jobs. Efforts were made to spread available work, and to arrange leaves of absence for those who found temporary jobs on farms or elsewhere, so their pension rights would not be lost. The old ball field was plowed up for garden plots for any of the shop men who wanted them, and William Delphia had a small nursery business there, selling shrubs and plants. The old hammer shop, now standing idle, was rented in 1933 to Christopher Swezey, Inc., for the manufacture of clothespins.

During World War II, the boys' camp and the tearoom both closed. The manufacture of garden tools was much restricted by shortages of steel, but the manufacture of snowshoes for the armed forces boomed. For a time there was a night shift, and the number of employees at the plant during those years went as high as 250. A new, automated brick sawmill was built in 1945.

TRUE TEMPER CORPORATION

By the time the war was over, a more conservative administration in the Cleveland office was running the company. They had decided that they were tool-makers and should stick to their trade, and had begun disposing of their other businesses and unused property as opportunity offered. In April of 1945, the boys' camp and the Stone Meadow south of Batcheller Field were given to Fire District No. 1, "to be used as a public park or playground, for the benefit of the public generally, and particularly of the residents of said Fire District." The snowshoe business, much depressed because of war surpluses, was sold to Raymond Taft, Jr., and moved from the "north shop" to its present location on Elm Street. In 1949, Mr. Treadway bought True Temper Inn, and its name was changed to Wallingford Inn. In 1951, the Ice Bed lot and two other pieces of woodland were sold for $243.60 to the federal government for inclusion in the Green Mountain National Forest. The old hammer shop was no more; it had been damaged by fire and its machinery salvaged for scrap during the war. Now the company owned nothing at the old Batcheller Works site, the office building on the hill having already been sold to be used as a residence.

July 1, 1949, the name of the company was changed to True Temper Corporation. This name caught on as American Fork and Hoe Company never had. Formerly one spoke of the shop, or the factory, but ever since the change it has been commonly referred to as True Temper.

In the early 1950's, Local No. 26 of the United Steelworkers of America was organized at the plant. What seems to be best remembered of its activities during its early years are the annual shop picnics at the boys' camp, sponsored jointly by the union and the company.

A drastic change in company operations came in 1956, when all forging and assembly of tools was discontinued, leaving only wood-working operations in Wallingford—the sawmill, and turning stock for handles. Once water power was superseded, this change was probably inevitable, because of the expense of shipping in both steel and coal. Another change came in 1967, but one that made little difference locally: True Temper Corporation was acquired by Allegheny Ludlum Steel Corporation. The announcement stated that True Temper would continue to operate under the current management and organization, but as a subsidiary of Allegheny Ludlum.

Managers during the years since the war have been Frank Miller, Lynn Davis who had spent part of his boyhood in Wallingford, Donald Keener, Paul Mooney, the only Wallingford native to hold the post, and Charles Sharp, the present manager.

The businesses that were spun off by True Temper have continued in independent operation. Miss Tarbell opened the Old Stone Shop to the public again after the war, but it was a gift and antique shop and no food was served. The morning of July 3, 1968, there was a fire which seriously damaged the building, especially the roof. The stock was saved by neighbors and passersby, and soon business was being carried on in the next-door barn. That fall True Temper deeded the building to Miss Tarbell. Repairs were completed during the winter, and since May 30, 1969, business has been carried on as usual at the Old Stone Shop during the summer months.

In 1951, a group of local people formed a corporation and bought the Wallingford Inn from Mr. Treadway; Mr. and Mrs. Clifford Gibson managed it for them until 1964, when the old landmark was purchased by Mr. and Mrs. Burley. Since July 7, 1968, the Inn has been the home of the English Language Center. Foreign students come here to prepare

Old Stone Shop, by Donald Wiedenmayer

themselves, in the English language, for entrance into colleges all over the United States. It started with 23 students from Canada and El Salvador. Others have come from Japan, Thailand, Venezuela, Colombia, Honduras, and Mexico. The Center is directed by Professor Ernest Boulay, the founder and former head of the Department of English at St. Michael's College in Winooski, and an expert in the teaching of English as a second language.

The snow shoe business gradually worked off the war inventory, and the company has continued to turn out large numbers of snow shoes. It has had a number of owners. Raymond Taft sold the business to Roger Maher, who ran it for several years. He sold it to a company headed by Finley Shepard of Wallingford. In 1958, Harold Underwood, Armand Richards, and Donald Coleman purchased it, and soon after, Harold Underwood became sole owner. He ran it until 1970, when the present owner, Baird Morgan, purchased Vermont Tubbs.

THE MARBLE QUARRIES and
WHITE PIGMENT CORPORATION

In South Wallingford, on the west side of Route 7, there is a vein of marble where three quarries once operated. The first, just north of the village, was opened in 1835 by Orange Carpenter and later was operated by Mr. Lippitt and finally by Mr. Kelley. A marble mill was built nearby, powered from a dam in Otter Creek. A second quarry, still farther north and called the Robinson Hall quarry, was opened in 1855. The third quarry, run by J. Adair and brother, was just south of the village and opened in 1857. The Adairs used the marble mostly for headstones, which they hewed and carved by hand. There was a dam in the creek near this quarry, built so that it could be used as a bridge, and ox teams drew marble blocks from the Adair quarry across it, through a saw mill yard to the East Road and to the finishing mill. Around 1864, Mr. Adair built a marble mill, but that business did not succeed. By the early 1900's, none of the three quarries was operating.

John R. Adair, son of the quarry owner, was proprietor of the Wallingford Monumental Works near the depot in Wallingford village. He started the business just after the Civil War and was at that same location for more than 40 years. He and his employees carved many of the gravestones in Green Hill Cemetery.

The abandoned Adair quarry was purchased by the White Pigment Corporation, which began operating there in 1954. The quarry supplies crushed marble, a limestone, which is trucked daily to the company's Florence, Vermont, plant. At this plant, the limestone is processed into a fine inert filler that is used by manufacturers of floor coverings, paint, plastics, paper, and for many other varied products. At the present time the quarry in South Wallingford employs 17 men.

POST OFFICES

The post office in Wallingford village was established in 1807. There is a list of the 24 people who have served as postmaster, but little information is available about the locations of the office during all those years. An 1869 map shows it on South Main Street at the home of Mrs. Bucklin, the postmaster. For many years it was in one or another of the village stores. A wall of wood and glass, with a service window and with open-ended boxes on the back, could be moved quite readily from one business establishment to another, depending on who was postmaster. The boxes were call-boxes, with no doors; a patron could see through the glass if there was mail in the box bearing his number, and ask for it at the window. Later, half of the store space in the Odd Fellows' block was rented, and a more substantial section of boxes, with doors secured by combination locks, was installed. Recently the post office has been moved to new quarters in Marvin Blanchard's complex at the northwest corner of Main and Elm Streets. Donald Shedd is postmaster.

South Wallingford's post office dates back to 1838. In the early years, Jacob Warner brought the mail on horseback; his route was from Rutland to Manchester. For a time, the mail came by the stage, which stopped at the tavern. After the railroad came through in 1852, mail came on the train and the post office was in the station. In 1908, Postmaster William Girard moved it to his store. Mrs. Mary Welsh succeeded him in 1942 and the office was moved to the Welsh home, where it now is. Mrs. Ruth Perry became postmaster when Mrs. Welsh retired in 1968.

The East Wallingford post office was established June 20, 1851, and Joel Constantine was the first postmaster. The location of the office during the earliest years is not known, but it was in John Priest's house above the tracks in the 1890's, and after that in the John Ridlon store across from the Baptist Church. For a time it was in a small building in the center of the village; this burned, and then, while Mrs. Nancy Graves was postmaster from 1945 to 1962, it occupied another small building on her property across from the schoolhouse. Since 1968, Mrs. Arlene Belcher has been postmaster and the office is neighbor to Cole's Trading Post in the building behind Hearthside Distributors.

All mail is now sent to and from the three post offices by truck. There are two rural routes. Miles Richards works out of the East Wallingford post office, serving the east side of town and into Mount Holly, and Charles Hager out of the Wallingford post office; he covers the Otter Creek valley, West Hill, and a part of Tinmouth.

STORES AND TIN SHOPS

The store in South Wallingford, presently known as Rowe's General Store, is believed to have been in operation as far back as 1813. Owners at one time were Ebenezer Towner and Mosley Hall, who also owned the two local taverns. There were other stores in the area and competition was keen. Clothing, hardware, and groceries were carried, and the store operators had their own chickens and cows to provide strictly fresh eggs and milk. Clerk Dyer Townsend not only waited on customers but also milked the cow and gathered the eggs. By 1852 the Rutland Railroad ran behind the store, and at least one of the store's many proprietors was also the station master. The present owners, who have been there for nine years, are Elmer and Clara Rowe.

The building on the southeast corner of Main and School Streets in Wallingford, now known as the Odd Fellows' Block, was built in 1824 by the partnerships of Button & Townsend and Johnson & Marsh.

Howard Harris accused them of forming an alliance to drive him, a new merchant, out of town. It has had a long succession of storekeeper tenants; an 1869 directory lists Edwin Martindale as proprietor. W. D. Hulett later owned and enlarged it, as he also enlarged the hotel across the way. W. P. Cary sold groceries in the north side and dry goods in the south side for many years in the early 1900's. Tenants who followed him included Ladabouche & Mooney, Bert McClure, Clarence Shedd, and Voluntine Rollins. The north side is presently occupied by the Wallingford Public Market and the south side is vacant. Just north of the building, where the School Street sidewalk runs now, there used to be a wagon scales, a heavy wooden platform set level with the ground, for weighing loads of hay and grain.

A small building formerly stood just south of the Odd Fellows' Block, and directly on the sidewalk. Luther Tower had a candy store there in the late 1800's. Heman Mandigo occupied it for a time after he retired from the fork factory; he repaired watches and clocks, fixed spectacles, and sold valentines in season, a business he later moved to his home on North Main Street. Arthur Babbitt started his plumbing and heating business there, and then moved to the Sabin building down the street; John Hoadley was in business with him for a time. The building was moved well back from the street, and is now used as a garage for the residence next door.

The original building on the northwest corner of Main and Depot Streets was a residence that had been moved there and used as a store. After it burned, in 1879, Justin Batcheller built the present building; many different businesses have occupied it. Around 1915, Will Hager kept a drug store in the north side; others carried on the business after him. Will Wilber ran it for a while, and later Mrs. Wilber and her sister continued it, first in the old bakery, then in the house on School Street just across from the Baptist church. Along with the stock of drugs, they had handmade baby things. (In the 1960's, Mrs. Winifred McClellan had a small drug store at her home on South Main Street, opposite Dr. Bashaw's office.)

In the south side of the Batcheller Block, John Wood had his coal business and other activities, including the ticket office when the buses began going through Wallingford. His brother, Fred, sold candy, newspapers, and sundries. Later they occupied the whole store. John Bove followed the Wood Brothers. In 1964, Irving Smith bought the building and a little later remodelled it for a village size supermarket. It is now Averill's Country Market.

Charles Claghorn bought John Hodgson's store on South Main Street, between the Library and the brook, in 1868. The small square addition on the north side was put on for the postoffice when he was postmaster. On the north wall, just below the eaves, he had his name painted, spelled out in large letters. In back of his store was his livery stable, and he drove the hearse, which belonged to the Cemetery Association for some of those years. Herbert Savery worked for him in the store, and around 1900 took over the business. He sold groceries and dry goods, and for a time advertised watches and jewelry. Mrs. Savery carried on the business for a year or two after his death in 1935. A restaurant and other tenants have occupied the building since, and it is now Warren Baker's real estate and insurance office.

Old Sabin Block

The Sabins for two generations had a tin shop in a building on the east side of Main Street next to Roaring Brook. There were a number of tin shops in the town at various times, and the kind of business they did changed; in the early years, tinware was made and sheet-metal work done. Later, when more manufactured items were available, the tin shops became hardware stores or plumbing and heating establishments. Part of the Sabin building was used by other merchants. Upstairs was a hall where village organizations had their meetings, and which was used briefly as a school room. The building burned in 1908 and was replaced by a smaller one which George Sabin and then Arthur Babbitt occupied. It is now the American Legion Building.

A. P. Stafford is listed as having a tin shop on Main Street in 1869. He retired soon after and sold the building, which was used by a succession of owners as residence, barber shop, and finally telephone office.

East Wallingford saw its greatest economic expansion in the second half of the 19th century. An 1869 map shows that E. A. Cutler and E. R. Allen had general stores above the tracks, and there was a shoe store on School Street. In 1883, F. O. Stafford had a clothing and general store. In 1884, John Priest took over the business of S. H. Stevens, probably where Mr. Cutler had been; he used the building as store and post office, and it was then a residence until the relocation of the road. About that time, Henry Duval had a meat market on School Street.

Jonathan Smead had a tin shop across from the Baptist Church, which he operated for more than thirty years, starting in 1866. John Ridlon operated a busy country store in the same building for some 25 years; he was followed by Erwin Burton, Louis Berger, and Ralph Dana. The building finally burned, and there is now a new house on the site.

The store with the longest history in East Wallingford is the one that Henry White built in 1866 at the corner of Main and School Streets, where customers are still being served. Proprietors who have kept shop there, usually a general store, include R. D. Bucklin, Jerome Converse, W. D. Hulett, W. R. Spaulding, Eitapence Country Store, John McCann, Ralph and Edward Dana. For a time, Paula Valar had her Bargain Box there, selling imports and clothing, especially ski things. It is now the Hearth and Cricket Shop of Hearthside Distributors, started by John and Marge Zecher in 1968-69. The business has grown rapidly, helped by the energy shortage and the high cost of fuel oil and electricity for home heating. They offer a wide variety of wood-burning stoves. Fireplace screens with glass doors in front, which can be closed when there is no fire and thus prevent heat loss up the chimney, are popular. A comparatively new and unique item is a prefabricated fireplace and chimney unit that can be installed in any house.

MAPLE SUGAR INDUSTRY

It takes from 30 to 40 gallons of sap to make a gallon of syrup. Sap for high quality maple syrup comes only from rock or hard maple trees. Favorable weather, when the sap runs freely and most of the best maple syrup is made, usually occurs in March and early April when there is freezing at night and thawing during the daytime.

In pioneer days, the trees were tapped and a wooden or metal spout driven in, from which was hung a sap bucket. The number of "taps" or holes depended on the size of the tree. The sap was gathered in a large tub carried on a horse-drawn sled. It was boiled down in cast-iron kettles holding from 40 to 60 gallons, which were hung over an open wood fire. Once boiling was started, it was necessary to keep the sap at a boil until it reached the consistency of syrup. It was not uncommon to continue boiling all night.

Sugaring-off parties were held during the late afternoons or evenings and attended by whole families. Refreshments were served, including doughnuts, popcorn, pickles, hard-boiled eggs, and of course some of the new syrup. Sometimes a little syrup would be cooked longer to make sugar on snow.

For many years, maple syrup and sugar were used as sweeteners because cane and beet sugar were scarce and much more expensive. Most farmers had a grove of rock maples (referred to as a "sugar bush") and produced syrup and sugar for their own use and for sale.

In the late 1880's sugar houses were built and sap was boiled in large pans called evaporators which had partitions built in to control the flow of the sap. What started as sap at one end of the evaporator would eventually be boiled down and drawn off as syrup at the other end.

In recent times, much of the labor of collecting the sap has been eliminated. Flexible conduit or pipe is now attached to the spout at each tree which has been tapped, and the sap flows by gravity to the holding tank outside the sugar house. Then for the heating, oil-fired burners are used instead of wood fires.

At Wallingford there used to be many farms where syrup was made, but now there are only a few. In fact, the only modern sugar house in Wallingford Township, making syrup on a commercial basis, is that of Karl Chapman in South Wallingford village.

*   *   *   *

As the years went by, more and more people made their living by other occupations than farming. An 1881 *Gazetteer* lists 23 carpenters and builders, among them Orvis McKnight of East Wallingford, who built houses both in East Wallingford and Wallingford, and also built Judge Button's new law office. Oscar Eddy built the marble mill, and the houses for the workers, at the first marble quarry opened up in South Wallingford, opposite the present post office. Austin Wellman was a carpenter and bridge builder. There were eight blacksmiths, six carriage manufacturers, four insurance agents. One skill less in demand than in the earliest years was surveying; old town records contain so many lists of surveyors that it seems almost every citizen must have been able to qualify, and of course when the town was being opened up there was a great demand for their services.

The maps in Beer's *Atlas of Rutland County* are most useful guides to the town's business and industry at the midpoint of its history. There is a map of the entire township, and detail maps and business directories for each of the three villages. A framed copy of the village maps hangs in the town clerk's office in the Town Hall. The maps show, of course, many of the earliest businesses that have continued through the years, and a considerable number of new ones, especially in the east part of town.

MILLS AND SHOPS

In Wallingford village, there were three enterprises along Roaring Brook during these years. The building shown on Beer's map as Bradford & Sons Tannery, on the south bank of the brook, burned. In 1876, Frank Johnson built a grist mill there, giving Mill Street its name. It was later used as a saw and planing mill, and a cider mill, and is said to have had a carpet-cleaning wheel. It had several different owners, was damaged in the 1927 flood, and was finally taken down soon after.

The Fargo & Stafford Sash and Blind Factory on upper School Street had been built before 1850; snow shovels were also made there at one time. It changed hands many times before Messrs. Fargo and Stafford owned it, and many times after. The Wallingford Products Co. (B. W. Aldrich of Aldrichville, H. B. Barden who had founded the Wallingford Manufacturing Co., and Clifford Barden) owned it in 1917. They deeded it to the American Fork & Hoe Co., who in turn sold it to the last owner, Charles Dutcher. In its later years it was mostly just a saw mill, but turned out various wooden items, including small souvenir baseball bats. It burned in 1923.

Frank H. Hoadley, a blacksmith by trade, came to Wallingford after the Civil War, and acquired the shop on School Street formerly operated by Edwin Green. He conducted a successful business in general blacksmithing and carriage making there until 1882. Then he was partner with A. Q. Adams in the manufacture of patent mopsticks, ice picks, window cleaners, and an improved snow shovel having a strip of metal along the edge for durability. The shovel was also made in a small size for children. In 1885, he purchased his partner's interest. To accommodate his growing business, Mr. Hoadley built a large two-story building next to Roaring Brook. A number of men were employed in the factory, and also on the road selling to jobbers. All were covered by liability insurance, unusual at that time. After Mr. Hoadley's retirement the building was used briefly as a plumbing shop, and around 1930 was moved to Prospect Street where it now serves Clifford Dawson as barn and storehouse. The safe which Mr. Hoadley used in his business passed to Charles Foote for the local telephone company, and has just now been promised to the library, where it will be used to store library records.

At the time that Mr. Hoadley went into business, Wallingford had two other blacksmiths. William Clark had a forge on Railroad Street, and Joseph Randall was located beside Roaring Brook and opposite the present Legion Building. Joseph Greeno owned the building later, made it into a residence, and built his blacksmith shop in back of the house. At one time the second floor of the original building was a hall where local organizations held their meetings. Victor Regimbald was the blacksmith at Aldrichville; when operations there were over, he moved to Wallingford and had a shop behind his home, the brick house opposite the Catholic church. (The house is now an apartment house.)

Near where the main street crosses Mill River in East Wallingford were a grist mill, a saw mill, and a blacksmith shop, that had been built around 1860 and soon became a part of the E. H. and B. W. Aldrich enterprise. In 1881, the Aldriches advertised as dealers in lumber, hardwood, chair stock, grain, flour, and meal. Land along the river has been washed away by floods, and buildings in that area damaged. Two buildings stand now between the store at the corner and the river. One, that is nearer the river and has been called the old mill, is an apartment house. The other, next to the store and sometimes called the new mill, was a grain, feed, and farm implement store in the early 1900's. Proprietors included F. O. Bolster, Will Spaulding, William Chambers, Carl White, then George Eldred for two decades, and Clarence L'Hommedieu. It has recently been occupied by Leo Farley, who has a business in artificial flowers and cemetery memorials.

Around 1900, James McGuirk had a grain mill, and a wheelwright, wagon, and blacksmith shop, on River Street just beyond the bridge. The larger shop building had been the Earl & Williams carriage and blacksmith shop; in the early 1800's it was operated by Dennis Sird, a wheelwright, and G. A. Spooner, a blacksmith from Mt. Holly. This shop later became a garage, and was finally dismantled; the Dubeau house now occupies the site. The former grain mill now has the Bargain Box on the first floor and an apartment on the second.

Stewart & Pelsue had a sawmill and factory in Centerville making tubs and boxes for butter and cheese. Hosea Pelsue ran it for a time, later it was listed as H. Pelsue & Son. It seems to have gone out of business before 1900; the mill pond remained and finally went out in the 1927 flood.

In South Wallingford, the Burns blacksmith shop shown on the Beers map was later used by Myron Roberts as a store, and is now the Garrow residence. In 1898, the sawmill in Aldrichville was moved down the mountain to a location near the tracks, and for some years after that B. W. Aldrich was a lumber dealer in South Wallingford.

INNS AND TAVERNS

The hotel in Wallingford has been mentioned earlier. South Walling-ford has an even older hostelry, on Route 7, said to have been built in 1792. Long ago it was a station where fresh horses were kept ready for the stage, which travelled the old stage road on West Hill, going from Bennington to Rutland. A 4th of July Ball was held there in 1865; the upstairs ballroom is now three bedrooms. The building has had many uses, hotel, tavern, and antique shop. The present owners, Mr. and Mrs. Herbert Barker, call it the Green Mountain Tea Room; they take over-night guests and serve breakfast, lunch, and tea.

E. A. Cutler built the East Wallingford Hotel in 1863, and it had a number of proprietors. Joel Todd especially promoted it as a place for summer visitors, promising romantic scenery, good fishing, "rooms and table fare not exceeded by any country hotel," and a good livery stable. After it burned in 1888, A. W. Duval built a smaller hotel opposite the depot, which was moved to the original hotel site next to the church when the road was relocated. That hotel also burned, and the fire house is where the hotels formerly stood.

The Albert Kelley house north of Wallingford village was an inn in the early days. There have been a number of taverns, often in homes. It is said that Lent Ives kept one when his house stood on Main Street, and that Ethan Allen was once a customer. The Mosley Hall Tavern was between South Wallingford and Wallingford, and Jonathan Thompson's on what was later the Rogers farm near the Tinmouth line.

During the late 1800's, Mrs. Charles Claghorn took boarders at her home on South Main Street, where the Bryce Towsleys live now. Drum-mers would stay the night, and then hire a horse and buggy from her husband's livery stable next door to call on their customers in neighbor-ing towns. One winter, three young men from Troy who were medical students at the University boarded with her. They did their studying there and went on the train to Burlington periodically for new assign-ments.

CHEESE FACTORIES AND THE OLD CREAMERY

In 1869 there was one cheese factory, Ainsworth & Congdon on Church Street in Wallingford. A number of other cheese factories were built soon after. Gleason & Chilson had one in East Wallingford in a building that was remodelled and is now used by the Masonic Lodge. Alvin Hawkins operated the former Anderson enterprise on Sugar Hill, and William Stone's was on Big Pond Road. Abraham Ames built the Pearl Cheese factory on the East Road in South Wallingford in 1873; that building went out in the 1927 flood.

In 1876 Martin Williams put up another building for a cheese factory in Wallingford, about opposite Ainsworth & Congdon. It was taken over in 1885 by the Brigham Company of Boston, who ran it as a creamery with A. W. Andrews as manager. The Brigham Company later became the Whiting Milk Company; John K. Whiting came to Wallingford on occasion in a chauffeur-driven Stanley Steamer.

The creamery processed the milk brought in by local farmers, plus the collection from their creamery in Tinmouth, brought over by wagon. The milk was either shipped to Boston or made into butter or cheese, depending on the market in Boston. As many as 100 to 150 cans of milk might be shipped on a given day, or 35 to 40 wheels of cheese made, or up to a thousand pounds of butter churned. The company also had a milk-collecting station in South Wallingford, originally a farmers' cooperative, that handled fluid milk only. R. O. Bugbee followed Mr. Andrews as manager of the creamery, and served until it closed around 1930.

Allen Burton bought the building and converted it to apartments; it was later used as a ski club. A fire did considerable damage and it stood empty for a time, then was used briefly as a residence. In 1972 it was taken over by a Rutland group and remodelled for a half-way house for alcoholics, called Serenity House.

Chapter 5
Business and Industry II
(Businesses Started Since 1900)

Wallingford was included in a suburban section of the *Rutland City Directory* in 1911 only. There is both a business directory and a directory of residents of the town. Some of the listings are for businesses no longer represented in the town, or even needed—a grist mill, an ice dealer, three livery stables, two wheelwrights. Among other listed occupations, older residents will remember Miss Anna Cole, seamstress, on School Street; Arthur Davenport, photographer, on Elm Street; and William K. Merriam, milk dealer, South Wallingford Road. Miss Ida Kelley is listed as a market gardener on Stafford Avenue; although Miss Kelley was gray-haired and lame, she raised a garden and sold vegetables and grated horseradish in the village. Will Rogers was a paper hanger; he brought his equipment to the house where he was working in one of those big handcarts with yard-high wheels, and expected the housewife to have flour paste made and ready for him.

Four physicians and surgeons are listed, Dr. S. D. Hazen in East Wallingford, and Doctors Sherwin A. Cootey, J. H. Miller, and W. E. Stewart in Wallingford, with their addresses and office hours. It is a matter of regret to many that the town has no doctor practicing here since Dr. Donald Bashaw gave up his office to serve in the Rutland Hospital emergency room.

Also listed in the directory of course, are many businesses continuing from an earlier day. To bring the record to the present, other enterprises founded more recently are added in the following pages.

THE SEWARD FAMILY ENTERPRISES

In 1904, Arthur B. Seward purchased the Joel Constantine farm. This farm was the first settlement in the East Wallingford village area. Then in 1938, Seward bought part of the nearby Jackson farm. These lands now comprise the overall Seward farm operation.

In 1916, Arthur Seward started a small creamery in a converted corn crib with less than 1000 square feet of floor space. Cream, separated at the farm, was delivered to the creamery by the farmers or collected and brought there by the Sewards. After being pasteurized at the plant, the cream was shipped by railroad to a Boston area dealer at Somerville, Mass. Arthur Seward served as their agent until 1936 when Roland Q. Seward took over and established the Valley View Creamery, now in its 40th year.

Originally there were nearly 100 operating farms in the town of Wallingford; now (1975) there are only 8. Farmers who separated the cream fed the skim milk to the hogs and calves and raised all of their own livestock; other farmers delivered whole milk to the various village cheese factories. Farmers no longer separate milk and so do not have skim milk to feed pigs. In fact, they apparently don't raise pigs any more. The last agricultural census did not report a single pig in the town of Wallingford.

Over a million pounds of dairy products were handled each year by the original small creamery. The creamery now has grown from less than 1,000 to nearly 30,000 square feet, and more than one hundred million pounds of milk and other dairy products are processed annually. Milk is collected in stainless steel bulk tank trucks from 178 farms in five Vermont counties and one New York county. The original corn crib building still stands surrounded by the additions made over the years.

In 1947, Seward's Dairy, Inc., was established on North Main Street in Rutland. This was followed by the chain of restaurants located in Rutland, South Burlington, Burlington, Barre, Ludlow, and Glens Falls, New York. Employment for the entire organization, headquartered at East Wallingford, is just over 200 full-time employees. Thirty of the employees are residents of Wallingford.

The complete line of dairy products is distributed throughout the six New England states and eastern New York state. Large transport tanks of fluid milk are delivered to processing dealers in southern New Hampshire and eastern Massachusetts. Milk and cream, 1/2 ounce creamers of the type used in restaurants, butter, ice cream mix, buttermilk, soured cream, eggnog, and cheese, are sold under the Seward Family name and under private label. Two million pounds of cottage cheese and a million pounds of cheddar cheese are produced annually. Wholesale shipments of cheddar cheese are made to stores, restaurants, delicatessens, gift shops, and cheese shops over a wide area. An extensive mail order business, especially heavy at Christmas, sees gift packages mailed to all 50 states and to 25 foreign countries, all sent from the East Wallingford post office.

In the late forties, the growing business was running short of water to cleanse the plant equipment and tank trucks. At that time, permission was obtained from the Federal Green Mountain Forest people to tap the outlet of Wallingford (Big) Pond, and three miles of 4-inch pipe was laid from there to the plant. Included were filter beds and a chlorinating plant. This project was then widely referred to as "Seward's Folly." However, the system was a success and delivers 500 gallons per minute of fresh cold water to the plant.

At first, cheese whey and other dairy plant wastes were disposed of by discharging into Mill River. Because it polluted the streams, this common practice could not be long continued. The delay and difficulties in finding a satisfactory alternative method of disposal nearly forced the Seward Creamery and a number of other cheese operations in the state to go out of business. Finally, in conjunction with the U. S. Department of Agriculture and especially the University of Vermont, a spray irrigation system was developed at a cost of more than a quarter of a million dollars. Over 125 acres of grazing and crop land are now sprayed with the effluent during the warm months, through three miles of 4-inch distribution pipe. As many as 100,000 gallons a day are disposed of in this manner. This is believed to be the largest spray irrigation system used by any dairy plant in the East.

During cold weather the whey and other plant wastes are impounded in a 12½ million gallon storage lagoon and held until the weather is warm enough to pump the effluent into the irrigation system. Although the Sewards are large landowners, none of their land nearby was suitable for a lagoon, and so it was necessary to purchase more. All in all, this was another expensive project, and if the fishermen could have had their way it would never have been completed. Before the lagoon was constructed, the effluent was still being discharged into the river during the wintertime. Whey is a high protein food, so during the winter the fish enjoyed it and grew fat. Consequently in the spring the fishing was better than it had ever been before—and better than it has ever been since.

THE FEED STORE to DAWSON'S INC.

In the early 1900's, there was a grain store on Church Street in the former cheese factory building. It was known as "The Feed Store," and was operated by John Burdick. He sold to the Davis Feed Company of Rutland, who rented it to Carl White. He ran it until the middle 1930's, when it was taken over by Arthur Dawson. He retired in 1947 and his son, Ashburn Dawson, continued to operate "The Feed Store."

In 1948, Ashburn Dawson bought from Joseph Carrara a building located about a mile north of Wallingford on Old Route 7; it had been used as a restaurant and filling station. The grain business was then moved from Church Street to the new location.

This was a time of change for grain dealers. With bulk deliveries for the large farmers, and with many of the small farmers going out of business, the future of the small grain dealer looked dismal. A search for another business was begun. Mr. Dawson purchased the coal business from John Bove. There was no fuel oil dealer in town; in fact, not much oil was being used as fuel in Wallingford. It seemed that the change from coal to oil as fuel was about to start.

Mr. Dawson signed a contract with Mobil Oil Company for a supply of fuel. Two 10,000 gallon storage tanks were purchased, and a new International fuel oil truck. The business started as A. A. Dawson & Sons. It was later changed to Dawson's Inc., and now operates under that name.

THE TELEPHONE COMPANY

Wallingford is known to have had telephone service about 1904 from the Rutland County Telephone and Telegraph Company. During the years 1932-47, C. N. Foote was President of the company and his wife, Mabel, Secretary and Treasurer. In 1947, H. J. Fletcher of Bethel, Vermont, purchased the company and ran it until 1965, when the present Continental Telephone Company of Vermont acquired control.

The first switchboard, commonly called an exchange, was located in what is now the home of Fred and Lois Thurlow, opposite the Town Hall. It was operated by Mrs. Winifred Saunders. It was next operated by Mrs. Walter Maranville and her family where they lived on Depot Street, and then at their home at 15 North Main. While at this location, the flood of 1927 occurred. Kitty Hebert Brown recalls that when she came to work as a relief operator, she picked up the headset to answer a call and the board was so busy her hand literally froze to the set and it had to be pried away.

The next move was across the street to the home of Ann Benson, in the house where Harley Weeks and his family live. Mrs. Benson was switchboard operator for more than thirty years. It was finally moved to the last location of the operator-manned switchboards, the house purchased by the Foote family from Carson Stewart; he had operated a barber shop in the front room of the house for many years.

The historian for the New England Telephone and Telegraph Company, Esme Smith, remembers the move to the "Barber Shop" very clearly, because one night they could not reach the operator in Wallingford from Rutland so they hurried down to see if the switchboard had burned up. They discovered Charles Foote in the process of moving the switchboard from the Benson house to the Stewart house in a wheelbarrow. He hadn't bothered to notify the Toll Center of his plans. They stayed to help him put the board back into service, and found that during the preliminary preparations for getting set up at the new location Mr. Foote had, with his bare hands, bent a cable around a corner and broken nearly all the wires inside the jacket of the cable.

Mrs. Benson continued as operator at the new location for a brief time, and was followed by Mrs. Hyzer. Shortly after that, Mrs. Rhoda Baker became switchboard operator and served for many years.

In 1964 a dial house was built directly back of the main building, and all phones were converted to dial. Mrs. Baker retired at that time. The only operators were in Rutland to handle emergencies and toll calls. Party lines were changed from as many as 20 customers to 10, and later Continental changed all party lines to a maximum of 4 people on a line.

During the years of the local operator in Wallingford, a long steady ring on party lines meant a disaster of some kind, generally fire. The operator got the call and notified the Volunteer Fire Department. After the siren was installed on the Town Hall, she had to notify the town office too. Once the siren sounded, every "drop" on the board would come down because citizens wanted the news. It is interesting to note that the Volunteer Fire Department had a similar warning device installed after the town changed to dial, with the siren activated from some of the firemen's homes.

While the Foote family ran the telephone company, bills were usually sent out in long-hand on a quarterly basis. This was changed to monthly billing about 1947 when the Footes sold the business. Mrs. Herbert (May) Brown worked in the billing department for 21 years. An addressograph was added to address the billheads, but the actual bill was still in long-hand with the toll tickets enclosed with each bill. This practice continued until the Continental System moved the billing office out of Wallingford to Liverpool, New York, where the bills were sent directly from a computer to the customer.

Because of the growth of the Wallingford exchange, the Continental Telephone Company built a new dial house south of Wallingford village in 1974 and moved in new electronic equipment to serve the town. The property which the company owns on Florence Avenue continues to be used as a warehouse for telephone supplies.

Through its Wallingford exchange, Continental Telephone Company also serves South Wallingford, the rest of the valley, and West Hill. East Wallingford and the eastern part of the town are also served by Continental, but through the Mount Holly exchange, and calls from East Wallingford to other parts of the town are toll calls.

INGALLS BAKING COMPANY

In 1909, Bennona Ingalls and his son Frank took over a small home baking business. The building and the one next door, formerly known as the George Tower premises, were rented from Mrs. Claghorn for a three-year period and then were purchased.

Bennona would deliver, and his wife Ella and Frank did the baking. He had two horses and a buggy, and would go to Middletown, Tinmouth, and Danby. In about 1912 his son Montie came to work also. All their baking was done by hand. As their business grew, they would put boxes of bread on the train.

In 1923 there was a fire which almost completely destroyed the building. It was rebuilt, and a big Peterson oven was put in which would bake 270 loaves of bread at a time. By this time thay had two trucks and would go south as far as Shaftsbury and to Rutland, Fair Haven, and Poultney. They delivered to East Wallingford and Mount Holly by car.

All the goods were made with whole milk, eggs, etc. The bread and rolls were wrapped by hand and tied with a string. In 1926 a machine was bought to wrap the bread. This was necessary as bigger companies were making a cheaper bread and competition increased.

The bakery employed about ten people, three of whom later had home bakeries of their own. Carl Buffum went to Manchester, Steve Baker to Middlebury, and Frank Fox runs his own bakery here in Wallingford.

By 1933 Frank Ingalls had died, Bennona was getting old, and his son Montie wanted to get out of the business. It was sold on January 18 to Levi Munson, Roland Merchant, and Horace Holden. Munson eventually sold out his share to the others. In November, 1938, there was another fire, this time from a faulty furnace. This terminated the 29-year old bakery business.

SHOPS AND STORES

Listed in the 1911 directory under the heading "Millinery and Fancy Goods," is the name of Mrs. F. V. McConnell; she had a shop in her home on South Main Street, next to the brook. She sold hats and also, if a customer thought her old hat still had some wear left in it, would freshen it up with a new flower or a bit of ribbon. Somewhat later than this, Mrs. Beryl Cole had a hat shop on School Street in East Wallingford.

Mrs. McConnell's house had been, years before, the home of Arnold Nicholson, who had a harness and saddlery shop there. Two harness shops advertised in the 1911 directory. C. H. Congdon, on Railroad Street in Wallingford, offered "harness and shoe supplies, repairing a specialty." Walter F. Colby had his shop for many years on School Street in East Wallingford. He made harness and sold robes and blankets, and did general repairing, which his advertisement stated would be promptly attended to. He was interviewed for *Vermont Life* in the fall of 1953, 88 years old and still working in his shop.

Guido Malcarne was a master craftsman in wrought iron work, and at first had a workshop in the former Savery store. In 1945, he built his own shop on old Route 7 near the Clarendon line, and lived there while designing and building a new home, the first in the area to have radiant heat. Colonial lighting fixtures, railings, fireplace equipment and accessories, were all made and displayed in the shop. Herbert Brown and William Herrick worked for him. He moved the business to Connecticut, and the shop became a restaurant, then a gift shop, and is now the Plainfield Ski Club.

Paul Cary had one of the earliest antique shops in town, and he also did furniture repairing. His business was in his home on Route 7 north of Wallingford village, and was marked by the display of a very old-fashioned doll carriage, which he purposely priced so high that no one would buy it. His sign read, Paul Cary - Fixer. In the 1960's, Phyllis Frew had the old tavern in South Wallingford for her antique shop, The Golden Eagle. For a time, Miss Mary Taylor had a small shop in her home at the corner of Meacham Street. Cornelia Tarbell has a few antiques among the modern things at the Old Stone Shop, and just down the street is Lynne Gallipo's Yankee Maid. The newest of the shops is in the old Button house, also on Main Street, James and Sandra Marquis's House of Yesteryear.

Robert's Beauty Shop was opened after World War II in the former bakery on Main Street by Robert Buck. Before his enlistment in the Navy, Mr. Buck was a model for Norman Rockwell and was portrayed as Private Willie Gillis on Saturday Evening Post covers. Since his marriage, his wife Natalie has operated the shop, now on North Main Street, and he has directed his interest toward a successful career in insurance.

Patricia Stewart has her shop, which she calls Pat's Beauty Shop, in her home on Nash Drive. It was started in 1967.

In 1935, Lenzy Baker bought the big old house on Depot Street that had been the home of the Frank Miller and Parmenter families. At that time he had his own five or six piece orchestra, and held public dances in his barn, with John Lancour calling the square dances; his was the first orchestra to be heard over Rutland radio station WSYB. When Mr. Baker returned from war service in the 1940's, he opened the general store which he continues to operate, along with a barber shop. He was interviewed recently for the *Sunday Rutland Herald*, as the proprietor of one of the last real old country stores in Vermont.

The Landmark Shop in South Wallingford was opened in 1958 by Mike and Miriam Roberts. They have hand-made leather goods, gifts, and maple products. In a way, their shop dates back to the time fifty or sixty years ago when Mr. Roberts' mother sold maple syrup and butternut fudge from a card table on the lawn of the family home; she was one of the first to make and sell the maple candy. And thirty-five or forty years ago, Mr. Roberts and his sister bought a road-side stand that had been used at the Ainsworth farm, moved it to their yard, and they too sold maple candy.

Also on Route 7 in South Wallingford, Karl and Gertrude Chapman have a gift shop and sell some of the maple products made in their nearby sugar house.

Norbert and Doris Cole keep the one grocery and general store currently operating in East Wallingford. Cole's Trading Post is on School Street, behind the Hearthside, and occupies a building which Carl Griswold reconstructed a few years ago from an old barn.

THE BUILDING INDUSTRY

When the population of the town was no longer increasing, there were fewer carpenters and masons; only six are listed in the 1911 directory. In the 1920's, Paul Thayer, an architect and builder, had a crew who put up many of the cottages near Elfin Lake. They were of rustic construction; the principal posts, studs, and beams were sections of trees of suitable size with the bark left on. Maple, cedar, or yellow birch was used; a few, very handsome, had white birch. Mr. Thayer also built the original Long Trail Lodge in Sherburne in the same way, using yellow birch.

Marshall Baker moved here from Danby and was a head carpenter; he and his sons, Sumner and Will, did most of the remodelling at True Temper Inn. George Stratton did the masonry work there, and George Fiske and Will Rogers the painting and paper hanging. John MacIntyre did the 1969 remodeling at the Library.

Among the other carpenters and painters who have worked in the community are Raymond Bouley, Clayton Doty, Fred Doubleday, Eugene Miner, Roy Patch, Wilbur Pelsue, and Louis Potter. Electricians and plumbers include Arthur Babbitt, Donald Coleman, Hazen Doubleday, James Ingalls, Robert Johnson, Elmer Orr, and Leo Westcott. Herve Turgeon operates the Green Mountain Dry Wall Company; his men work wearing adjustable stilts. Excavating has been done by John Blanchard, Clyde Patch, and Edward Patch. Present-day housebuilders include Sherwin Fish, Richard Frederick, Raymond Guynup, and Lee Houghton.

GARAGES AND GAS STATIONS

At a home talent minstrel show presented some time in the 1920's, one of the end men is said to have asked the other, "Who put the ford in Wallingford?" and the answer came back, "Harry Townsend." Mr. Townsend first had a grain and feed business on Depot Street; around 1912 he added a Ford sales and service agency, and when it was clear that cars were here to stay he dropped the grain business. He had one of the largest Ford dealerships in the area, and also sold and serviced Hudson and Essex cars. Along with selling the cars, Mr. Townsend taught the new owners to drive them. He serviced all of the local Ambulance Company's vehicles. Gas pumps were up on Main Street, and customers rang a bell to call for service. Among his long-time employees were Carlos Williams, Elizabeth Pickett, and Howard Smith.

Townsend's Garage. L. to R., Dan Regimbald, Hugh Regimbald, Frank Murray, Carlos Williams.

For some years after Mr. Townsend discontinued the business, the former garage housed the high school shop. Presently, Mr. Townsend's son Frederick has an antique shop there, and also stores the antique fire engine that he drives in parades. Other tenants in the building are Carl Buffum's pottery studio, and Mike's foreign car repair shop.

Victor Regimbald, Jr., had a garage on Florence Avenue when cars first became popular. C. W. Towsley & Son later operated the garage and a Chevrolet agency. In 1937, Ransom Towsley moved the gas and oil business to Main Street and Hull Avenue. In recent years, the Main Street building has been rented to other businesses; it is presently a Lehigh station. The Towsleys continue to operate the Laundromat on Hull Avenue, which they established in 1962 because so many tourists stopping for gas inquired about where they could get laundry done. (Levi Munson started a laundry in the early 1920's, but continued it only a short time.) Mrs. Towsley has a small business in ceramic figurines of the Boy with the Boot, and models of the little red schoolhouse, the present Rotary Building.

Also in 1937, part of the old ball field was sold for the Gulf station now operated by Francis Shaw. Mr. Shaw has another business, Wallingford Gas and Oil, and distributes fuel oil, kerosene, and bottled gas. Around 1940, the Crary house was set aside (and later made into apartments) to make room for the Texaco station which Marvin Blanchard now operates, along with his store and real estate business, at the corner of Main and Elm Streets. Albert Bersaw built his Exxon station between Wallingford and South Wallingford in 1950.

From 1919 to 1941, Leo G. Benjamin ran a garage, service station, and auto repair shop on School Street in East Wallingford. For the next twenty years he operated a tool distributing center there. He is retired now, but still owns the property.

Wade's Auto Service is on the Weston Road, also in East Wallingford.

For some years now, John Perry has had a garage and repair shop on Route 7 in South Wallingford.

Wayne Jones came to Wallingford in 1962 and started a business on Hull Avenue, which he later moved to North End Drive. Recently Wayne's Body Shop moved once more, to a newly renovated building at the corner of River Street and Elm Street Extension.

INSURANCE

The Rural Cooperative Insurance Company was organized in September, 1933, by Charles Foote. It was the third of three such companies, the other two having been organized in Middlebury by Mr. Foote's father, Abram Foote. The purpose was to offer at the lowest possible cost fire and lightning protection, up to $12,000, to Vermont farmers; an eligible applicant could take out $4000 of insurance in each company.

The first president was Donald Leach, who served until his death in 1967; for many years he operated a dairy farm just south of Wallingford, and peddled milk in the village. Charles Foote was the first secretary, and the office was in his home on Main Street until December, 1945, when he resigned for reasons of health; then the office was moved to the Town Hall. Clarence J. Wilbur succeeded Mr. Foote as secretary.

In 1952 the three companies were joined to form the Cooperative Fire Insurance Association of Vermont, with the home office in Middlebury and Donald Leach as president. Policies are now written from there although an office is still maintained in Wallingford, as required in the By-Laws. It is presently at the home of Margaret Davenport on Waldo Lane.

There are also agencies of national insurance companies here. Ralph Stafford, the town's representative in Montpelier, has an office at his home in South Wallingford. Warren Baker and Clifford Dawson both have combined insurance and real estate offices in Wallingford village.

FOX'S HOME BAKERY

Fox's Home Bakery was started during the depression of 1938 with 24 lbs. of flour, 6 bread tins, and a small kitchen range. Frank Fox, the owner, was unemployed at the time, having been laid off from work at the United Baking Co. in Center Rutland. The idea of working for himself was suggested one day when Mr. D. C. Marble asked Frank to bake six loaves of bread for sale in his store, which was located next door to the Gilbert Hart Library. A hand mixer that mixed eight loaves at a time and a small oven were purchased as a beginning. One year later the bakery was moved to the basement of the Fox family home, its present location.

It is interesting to compare costs of materials and of bakery products when Frank started in business with what they are now.

	1939	*1975*
Flour	— 2¢ per lb.	14¢ per lb.
Yeast	— 18¢ per lb.	67¢ per lb.
Sugar	— 6¢ per lb.	69¢ per lb. (during shortage)
		24¢ per lb. (later in year)
Bread	— 10¢ per loaf	59¢ per loaf
Rolls	— 12¢ per dozen	65¢ per dozen
Doughnuts	— 40¢ per dozen	$1.50 per dozen

The Department of Agriculture recently stated that there are 153 hidden taxes in one loaf of bread.

Today Fox's Home Bakery is a wholesale and retail operation serving about 17 stores in Rutland, Danby, and Wallingford. This small successful home industry is carried on entirely by Mr. and Mrs. Fox and one part-time employee. Bread, rolls, doughnuts, and cookies are standard products. Pies, cakes, and other bakery goods are made to order. At Christmas time cookies are shipped to different parts of the United States, especially (a favorite) Vermont Molasses Cookies.

BORDEN'S

Borden's was built in 1940 by C. J. Fayen on land purchased from the American Fork & Hoe Company. Mr. Fayen operated a milk receiving station for several years, and then sold out to the Borden Company who operated a creamery for a short time. They ceased operations because of a short supply of milk. The building was then leased for the manufacture of clothespins for a little over a year. After standing idle for several months, it was converted to an ice cream distributing plant. At the present time, Richard Belden leases it from Borden's and operates it.

WALLINGFORD LOCKER

In 1944, a group of residents led by Ralph Congdon and Charles Foote organized a cooperative frozen food locker. They borrowed $13,000 from a cooperative bank in Springfield, Mass., and renovated and insulated the building on Florence Avenue that had been Towsley's Garage. Fred Cox was manager until 1952; others were Royal Thayer, Edgar Stevens, and Gordon Stewart. Customers rented lockers, and could have a side of beef or a deer cut up; some frozen food and a little meat were sold over the counter. The organization disbanded in 1961, and those who had invested received their money back.

The Courcelles from Rutland acquired the building in 1961, and have enlarged and improved it. The addition made to the plant included a smoke house where their famous cob-smoked hams are cured and smoked. Besides renting the lockers, they do a considerable meat business, both wholesale and retail, and are widely known for their quality products and courteous service.

THURLOW SALES AND SERVICE

Fred Thurlow started a general plumbing and heating business on River Street in 1946, and moved to the former feed store on Church Street in 1947 to obtain more room. (That building has been remodelled and is now the home of Stanley Stewart.) Then in 1949, Fred and Lois Thurlow purchased the property at 12 School Street which has been the business home ever since.

The plumbing and heating business in this period was changing fast. Oil and wood burning stoves and furnaces were being replaced by automatic oil furnaces. Better ways were being found to supply domestic hot water. Deep wells were drilled and electric pumps installed to provide water as the supply from springs became inadequate. New sewage disposal systems often were required.

In the early 1960's, the power company was promoting the sale of electric heat. One effect of this was to promote the insulation business, which Fred decided to enter. He formed the Thurlow Insulating Corporation and rented Hugh Young's barn on South Main Street to provide storage space for the insulating materials. Then in January, 1973, this business was sold. Finally, in November 1974, Fred Thurlow and Bernard Nash formed a real estate agency which is their present business.

VERMONT PAVING CORPORATION
VERMONT SAND & GRAVEL CORPORATION

These plants are located on what used to be the Lawrence O'Brien farm and on land purchased from Charles Tarbell. Building was started by the Frank W. Whitcomb Construction Corporation in 1966, and the plants were in full operation in 1967. Since then they have supplied hot mix and cold patch to towns, cities, the state, and individuals, as well as material for their own contract jobs. Whitcomb Construction did the paving on Route 7 access roads and most of the paving on Route 4. During the active season—spring, summer, and fall—the Wallingford plant employs approximately 25 people.

This Construction Corporation was formed by Frank W. Whitcomb in 1932, and since that time has grown to be among the larger firms of its type in New England. In addition to Wallingford, the corporation operates plants in Burlington and Winooski, Vermont, and in Walpole and Keene, New Hampshire. It paves a substantial number of highway miles each year in Vermont and New Hampshire.

TUCKAWAY TRAVEL TRAILER PARK AND CAMP GROUND

In 1969, Mr. and Mrs. William Burke Miller drove to the West Coast with their trailer. During this lengthy trip, and others, they had visited many trailer parks. When they returned home, they decided to create a really good park, based on their experience in trailer park living. Their land provided a pleasant location, with ample space, trees, and a brook. It is in South Wallingford, just off Route 7.

After some difficulties about permits, about a water supply, and about signs, the park was opened in August, 1969. There are 18 drive-through sites so no backing is required, a dumping station, a road all the way through the park, water and a sink drain and electricity at each site. Later, a dozen tent sites were built in a camping area up in the woods. The sites are never all in use at the same time. The Millers have been pleased with their guests, and a number of them have already bought, or are looking for, a house or a piece of property in this part of the country.

OTHER BUSINESSES

Fifty years ago boarding houses were common; men and boys who came to work at the fork factory used to live at Minnie Hill's, at the corner of Main and Mill Streets. There were farms, like the Rogers farm, that catered to summer visitors, some of whom returned year after year. These, and the hotels, have been replaced by an increasing number of apartments, and by family enterprises that take a few guests, like the 8TN Lodge on Main Street. The earlier ones took "Tourists," or the overflow from True Temper Inn during the foliage season; now the sign is likely to say "Skiers."

Elizabeth's Pub, next to the library, is the only tavern in town. Its new proprietor is Charles Wallis; Mrs. Wallis writes books for children and young adults under the name of Hope Campbell. The building that houses the Pub has a long history. For 98 years, from 1830 to 1928, it was the Congregational parsonage. Then, in order, it was D. C. Marble & Son's grocery store, the Mayflower Restaurant, the Cork and Kettle, and, three or four years ago, Elizabeth's Pub.

Not strictly a business but an interesting enterprise in the community is Kinavik Kennels. For eleven years Mr. and Mrs. Dennis Kitchin have been raising and racing Siberian Huskies and Alaskan racing dogs; they brought their hobby with them when Mr. Kitchin, who works for the Forest Service, was transferred to this area. He is president of the New England Sled Dog Club. He races, as a professional, all over New England, driving a team of seven to ten dogs, the number depending on the length of the race and the difficulty of the terrain. Kinavik, the name they use, is an authentic Eskimo word meaning a refuge or haven—an igloo, but the kind an Eskimo would build for shelter in a blizzard, not one to live in.

There are other interesting one-of-a-kind projects in the community. P. J. Bushey has established a landscaping business on the former Peter Pelkey farm in East Wallingford. Alton Barrows has an Auction Barn in South Wallingford, and in the summer he conducts weekly auctions. Bernard Bigelow is president of Babco Communications, started a year and a half ago in the former Inn garage on Taft Terrace; they set poles and run lines for the telephone and the power and light companies.

*   *   *   *

Just a mention was found of other enterprises—stages that ran between Tinmouth and Wallingford, and between East Wallingford and Cuttingsville over Hateful Hill; teamsters who took produce and lumber to Albany or Boston before the railroad came through; a sawmill on Roaring Brook beside Route 140, the remains of the dam still there; and another sawmill and tray factory in the very south east corner of the town. No doubt there are others, but all the economic enterprises about which information was forthcoming have been included in these two chapters on Business and Industry.

Chapter 6

Organizations

Park Association
Maple Valley Grange
Green Hill Homemakers
4-H Clubs
Boy Scouts
Girl Scouts
Youth Community Center
Bear Mountain Pioneers
Parent Teacher Association
W. H. S. Alumni Association
Taxpayers' Association

D. A. R.
G. A. R. and Women's Relief Corps
American Legion and Auxiliary
Ambulance Company
Civil Defense Police Unit
White Rock Fish and Game Club
White Rock Riders
Masons and Eastern Star
I. O. O. F. and Rebekahs
Rotary

THE WALLINGFORD PARK ASSOCIATION

This association was incorporated on April 22, 1919, for the purpose of accepting a gift of land for the Park. The Subscribers were H. B. Barden, A. W. Ferguson, R. C. Taft, George Batcheller, and Rev. O. R. Houghton.

On April 28, 1919, Lucretia Kent Stone deeded to the Association 30 acres of land, more or less, lying between Otter Creek and Elfin Lake to be known as the "Addison G. Stone Memorial Park." It was there that the pageants of 1911 and 1912 had been held.

Developments at the Park have included picnic tables and fireplaces, bathhouse, float, and refreshment stand. Later additions to the Park playground area included a jungle gym, swings, space for volley ball, basket ball, horseshoes, and a water slide. Many loads of sand have been drawn in to extend the beach inland and out into deeper water. For some years no fees were charged and no supervision was required. Then as attendance increased, particularly by people from out of town, a full time lifeguard and caretaker was hired for the summer months, and a fee was charged for admittance to the beach and swimming. Red Cross swimming lessons are given every summer for children of the village.

On September 10, 1929, about 4½ acres on the south side of Tinmouth Road, between the railroad and Otter Creek, were acquired by public subscription, through the efforts of W. P. Cary, for a recreation park. A baseball field was constructed thereon, and named Batcheller Field because the cost of labor and the many hundred yards of fill required to make a suitable athletic field were donated by Birney Batch-

Elfin Lake and the Park, by Donald Wiedenmayer

eller. Some years later two tennis courts were built, and in the winter these were flooded to provide a skating rink.

In 1973, a recreation program was begun which offered a varied morning program throughout the summer months including kickball, volleyball, softball, tennis, basketball, cycling, canoeing, camping, field trips, and arts and crafts. In 1974, a portion of the area was completely resurfaced to provide two regulation tennis courts, a basketball court, and driveways. Also in that year, a tennis instruction program for children, youth, and adults was begun.

In 1975, part of the adjacent Stone Meadow was leased from the Town and a ball field was laid out in that area, making a total of three ball fields of varying sizes available to the townspeople. A full Little League, Babe Ruth League, and Men's Softball League have kept the ball fields in constant use.

MAPLE VALLEY GRANGE #318

The Maple Valley Grange was organized at a meeting of the Patrons of Husbandry on December 8, 1903. There were sixty-three charter members, and George Kelley was the first Worthy Master.

The Grange met in Ladies Aid Hall until 1910 when the Grange Hall was built on land purchased from Mrs. Sarah Aldrich. The members of the Committee in charge of this project were Mr. and Mrs. George Stratton, Mr. and Mrs. D. A. Maxham, Mr. and Mrs. C. B. Stafford, Mr. and Mrs. J. N. Brown, and Mr. M. H. Roberts.

Volunteers helped in building the Hall, and many fund-raising projects were held. The first Grange meeting held there was on February 1, 1910 with Myron H. Roberts as Worthy Master.

The Grange has worked for issues concerning the advancement of farming on the national, state, and community level. It is still active today at the Grange Hall in South Wallingford.

GREEN HILL HOMEMAKERS—
RUTLAND COUNTY EXTENSION SERVICE

The Wallingford Home Extension program was started about 1925 by Mrs. James Safford, who continued as president until 1940. The group meets monthly, having programs on subjects of interest to homemakers, such as health, safety, crafts, sewing, food and nutrition, home management, and enrichment of daily living. Members usually provide material for the programs; some are group efforts with all sharing, some are a presentation by one or two members who offer information and expertise either from their own experience or from county-wide Extension Service meetings which they have attended. Sociability goes along with this exchange of ideas and information, and some meetings are entirely recreational—a picnic, a trip to see a play, a Christmas party.

Projects are also undertaken by the Homemakers. Health clinics have been conducted, trees planted, picnic tables provided, and contributions made to various community projects. The elderly and sick are remembered, especially at Christmas, with cards and gifts. A most important project each year is Operation Gift Lift for the State Hospital in Waterbury.

The Homemakers strive for character and leadership formed in family life, and have a good time doing it. The present membership is a cross-section of the women of the community.

4-H CLUBS

Otter Valley

This 4-H Club was organized in October, 1962, under the leadership of Helen Whipple and Virginia Stafford. Fifteen girls were enrolled from Wallingford, South Wallingford, and Danby. Their projects included sewing, cooking, crafts, health standards, and photography; they also did community service work.

During the ensuing years Carolyn Patch, Joyce Winship, Shirley Graves, and Janet McKinstry served as project leaders, aided in fund raising, and assisted at county events. Junior leaders who contributed to the success of the Club included Anne Hager, Debra Bartlett, Faye Graves, Connie Stafford, Janice Stafford, Dawn Winship, Tina Graves, Judy Baker, and Rhonda LaFrancis. These girls were also active in yearly county events.

Each year several members participated in the County Style Review, where they modeled clothes they had made. Some were chosen to attend the State Style Show in Barre. The Club also participated in the Cherry Pie Contest, and 4-H Foods Day, held in Rutland. Many of the members were exhibitors in the 4-H Department at the Rutland Fair, and for several years had a Club project on display. During the ten years of Club activities, three members were eligible for the 4-H State Honorary Society, and two members were selected, on the basis of records and personal interviews, to attend the 4-H Club Congress in Chicago.

Groovy Gallopers Horsemanship

In February, 1972, Alfred St. Onge and Mrs. William Graves organized this Club. It started with nine members; by 1975 the membership had grown to around thirty. Members are taught to ride and to care for horses, and they participate in Trail Rides, overnight camping, and Gymkhanas.

In 1974 a large arena was built on St. Onge land for the use of all members. Two members, Tina Graves and Michael Sheehe, rode in the Vermont State Gymkhana in 1974, and also entered a horse at the Rutland Fair Horse Show.

BOY SCOUTS

The Wallingford Boy Scout Troop 12 of Green Mountain Council was first chartered on September 30, 1933 by a Town Committee composed of Harry Townsend, Charles Danolds and Charles Foote with Scout Masters Clifford Stevens and Earl Reynolds. It was reorganized in 1941 under the sponsorship of the Modern Woodmen of America, Elfin Lake Camp No. 11139. The troop committee consisted of Frank Fox, Levi Frederick, Ernest Lidstone and Bert Fox, secretary of the Modern Woodmen.

Troop 12 is now sponsored by the Ralph H. Pickett Post No. 52 of the American Legion and a group of interested citizens. Some of its projects have been an annual Christmas wreath for the Library door, Christmas baskets to some of the elderly in town, and setting out trees in Elfin Lake Park.

The Troop maintained a spring on the Long Trail for years. It was brought to the attention of the Scouts when Antonio Petraglio was scoutmaster and George Holden, assistant scoutmaster. At this spring, Mr. Petraglio, as a boy, gathered water while working at cutting the timber on White Rocks. The spring is listed in the Long Trail Guide Book. The Boy Scouts at one time kept a note book in a glass jar for all who passed by to sign. It was interesting to read the names and comments of those who appreciated the nice cold drink of water.

Troop 12 has had three Eagle Scouts: Herbert Brown, Jr., Wallingford; Warren Hedding, Tinmouth; Jonathan Houghton, Wallingford; four Life Scouts and seven Star Scouts plus many in first and second class ranks. Some Scouts have attended Camp Sunrise or Camp Plymouth each year. Four boys have been to Philmont Ranch in New Mexico.

GIRL SCOUTS

The first Girl Scout troop in Wallingford was organized in 1939 by Mrs. Margaret Baker and was active for three or four years. Then in 1956 Mrs. Leona Fish started a new troop and together with eight other women took a leadership training course in Rutland. Since that time there has been at least one, and as many as five, troops of girls, covering the four levels of Girl Scouting—Brownies, Juniors, Cadettes, and Seniors. There is no Senior troop at this time.

Many girls over the years have participated in day camps and overnight camps sponsored by the Vermont Girl Scout Council. These troop campouts, cookouts, and hikes have added variety and interest to the program while the girls were learning new skills and earning pins and badges. The Girl Scouts also participate regularly in various service projects such as "clean up" days, visits to nursing homes, and baby sitting during Town Meetings.

Present troop leaders are: Brownies, Alberta Armstrong; Juniors, Barbara Davenport and Jaye LaFrancis; Cadettes, Lois Randolph; Coordinator for Troop Activities, Alberta Armstrong.

YOUTH COMMUNITY CENTER

In 1964 the town voted the South Wallingford Youth Community Center the use of the Little Red Schoolhouse for community activities to be used at no cost to the town.

Little Red Schoolhouse, by Donald Wiedenmayer

Several months later the Center was incorporated with eleven directors on the board. Seven of the original directors are still serving—Madge and Burke Miller, Rev. Richard Armstrong, Karl Chapman, Laszlo Kerr, Charles Rist, and Frank Stafford. A year later four more directors were added and fifteen directors have functioned since then.

The first use of the Center was on Mother's Day, 1964. The 4-H Club of Wallingford entertained their mothers. The first children's play "Snow White and Rose Red" was in June when for the first time we proudly used our first—and present—stage curtain. The first Children's Fair, the brain-child of Helen and Thayer Jaccaci, took place in July.

In the intervening years there have been many 4-H and Girl Scout meetings, birthday parties, showers for brides, receptions, business meetings, Grange meetings, more than a hundred plays, a Puppet Theater, movies, craft projects, teen dances, Easter Egg Hunts and board meetings.

Hundreds of adults as well as hundreds of children have participated; have come to the fair, bought raffle tickets, baked cookies, joined the car pool, made costumes, found treasures in attics, painted the building inside and out, built playground equipment, made posters, worked in the fair, painted and papered scenery, joined the clean-up squad, contributed to and bought The Little Red Schoolhouse Cook Book, and lent moral support.

BEAR MOUNTAIN PIONEERS

The Bear Mountain Pioneers were organized by "Chuck" Wade, and held their first meeting on February 16, 1969, in Chuck's car. Officers elected at that meeting were Chuck Wade, President; Norm Shum, Vice-President; Neil Patch, Secretary; Norm Coote, Treasurer. Others present were Roger Smith, Mike Holland, and Kevin Reed.

Activities included hiking, camping, field trips, tours, community projects, and fun. The organization was self-supporting and over a four year period raised around $2700 through dues and various projects including raffles, auctions, and bingo. In no year did their expenditures exceed their income.

Club jackets were red with white insignia and were worn on special occasions such as parades; twenty-two members marched in the Veterans' Day Parade on October 25, 1971.

Among the community projects of the Bear Mountain Pioneers were placing a lighted Christmas tree on the lawn by the English Language Center, and conducting several "Clean Sweep" projects. Streets with curbs were swept, and litter was picked up along other streets in the village.

WALLINGFORD PARENT TEACHER ASSOCIATION

In response to a call from the (then) Superintendent of Schools, Miss Mary Murphy, thirty interested people met on June 1, 1923, and formed the Wallingford Parent Teacher Association. The first officers were: President, Mrs. C. N. Batcheller; First Vice-President, Mrs. Fay Dean; Second Vice-president, Mrs. Porter Benson; Treasurer, Mrs. Victor Regimbald; Corresponding Secretary, Miss Stella Wooster; Recording Secretary, Mrs. Paul Thayer.

The Wallingford PTA has always been a local unit of the Vermont Congress of Parents and Teachers, and the National Congress of Parents and Teachers. By 1925 there were 160 members. It has been instrumental in raising funds and developing many and varied programs.

The Association has several "firsts" in its history. Early in its work it raised money for the first music teacher. During Mrs. George Fiske's term of office (1927-28) the PTA sponsored the first physical examination for all the school children. The first dental clinic sponsored by the Association was held in 1931 when Mrs. R. C. Taft was President. May, 1936, saw the beginning of the pre-school clinics.

The PTA has sponsored many other projects—promoted the hot lunch program, made costumes for school operettas, made popcorn for the children's Christmas parties, sent a girl to Girls' State, paid dues for Junior Red Cross, bought two pianos, bought silver and dishes for the Home Economics rooms, and has given generously to many causes on a local, state and national level. In 1944 it bought additional acreage in the rear of the school building for a play ground, and later purchased playground equipment.

The PTA sponsored the bands until they became part of the school system in 1969. In 1951, it raised money for a band, bought material and made new uniforms. Because of lack of continuing student talent and adequate instruction, this lasted only a few years. In 1964, after about a ten year lapse a band was again started by the PTA and a director and instructor was engaged. Money earned from concerts, food sales, suppers, and donations from other organizations and citizens helped pay for the larger instruments and for new uniforms.

The Wallingford Parent Teacher Association has truly tried to live up to its objectives—to promote the welfare of youth in the home, school, church, and community.

WALLINGFORD HIGH SCHOOL ALUMNI ASSOCIATION

The High School Alumni Association was organized in 1955, and on Alumni Day 1956 held a big parade with more than 40 floats. The winning float was entered by the class of 1947 in memory of classmate

Maynard Lindsey, who was killed in an automobile accident. His father, Walter K. Lindsey, was principal of the high school at the time.

Mrs. Julia Newton Batcheller, a graduate of the first class in 1877, was honorary marshal. Other members of early classes riding in this first parade were: 1893, Mrs. Arthur Hughes; 1895, Aldace Newton and Fred Cook; 1896, Mrs. Aldace Newton; 1905, Irving Andrews; 1909, Paul Cary, Earl Stafford, Mrs. Hazel Jones, and Miss Mildred Ainsworth; 1918, Mrs. Barney Wetherby; 1919, Miss Mildred Ward and Mrs. Dorothy Eisenhart; 1920, Mrs. June Tarbell Smith and Mrs. Esther Merchant. The day was climaxed with a supper at the Boys' Camp, followed by a dance attended by more than 500.

Prize-winning float, 1975 parade—L. to R., Bryce Towsley, Ramona Wade, Richard Kennedy, Gordon Holden.

There have been many Alumni Day parades since then; the most recent, June 21, 1975, was planned as a salute to Wallingford High School, which had just graduated its last class. The winning float was by the class of 1949 and displayed the original bell that had been on top of the school house since about 1865. Mrs. Mildred Lidstone, a teacher at W. H. S. for 40 years, was honored in the parade, as was Mrs. Ruth Patch Aitken, who wrote the words of the Alma Mater. The Wallingford High School Band led the parade and played the Alma Mater in this, its last appearance.

WALLINGFORD TAXPAYERS ASSOCIATION, INC.

On May 26, 1970 a group of Wallingford residents met at the Rotary Building to discuss formation of a taxpayers' association which would gather information regarding the use of town tax money. At this meeting it was decided to organize and officers were elected as follows: Selden Rapelye, President; William Dolt, Vice-President; William Parker, Treasurer; Madeline Holden, Secretary.

Although the association soon grew to more than a hundred members, it was only active for a little over a year and became officially defunct on April 1, 1973 when it failed to file its annual report with the Secretary of State. Activities and accomplishments during that time included: maintaining auditors at meetings of the School Board, the Selectmen, and the Prudential Committee; adoption of the use of the Australian ballot in voting on the school budget; increasing the School Board from three to five members; and a wider interest in tax accountability on the part of both town officials and citizens.

In 1975 the directors voted unanimously to turn over the less than one hundred dollars left in the treasury to the Wallingford Bicentenial Committee.

DAUGHTERS OF THE AMERICAN REVOLUTION

In October, 1902, Mrs. Mary Fletcher Waldo, assisted by Mrs. Estey, then State Regent, organized in Wallingford the Palestrello Chapter of D. A. R., naming it after the wife of Christopher Columbus.

In an article in the July-August, 1914, issue of *The Vermonter*, D. A. R. Historian Julia E. Wilkins says of the chapter: "It has been greatly favored in its regents and the harmony and co-operation of its members. Its meetings every month in the year are well attended, and a literary program is followed by a social hour and refreshments much enjoyed."

A monument of white Vermont marble was dedicated by the chapter on August 15, 1914, to the memory of the Revolutionary soldiers from Wallingford. It stood directly over an ancient highway that was once the main road for moving freight from this section to Boston. This location is now the north lawn of the Congregational Church on Route 7, where the stone still stands.

During the second quarter of the 20th century, the Wallingford chapter took an active part in the social and patriotic functions of the town. To raise money for its projects, a card party was held each summer at the True Temper Inn; these parties were a regular feature of the social season, which in those days brought together year-round inhabitants, casual summer visitors, and the part-time residents who called the town "home" if only for a few months each year. It participated in the parades and patriotic observances on Memorial Day, July Fourth, and Armistice Day. Each year at the Commencement Exercises of the Wallingford High School, the national D. A. R. Good Citizen Award was bestowed on an outstanding Senior girl.

For many years an exhibit of D. A. R. memorabilia was on display at the Gilbert Hart Library. Here could be seen all kinds of mementoes ranging from Revolutionary relics to more recent items associated with D. A. R. and town history. In 1972, pertinent items from the exhibit were given to the John Strong Mansion, the D. A. R. Museum in Addison. Palestrello chapter was disbanded at that time, and Wallingford members may now belong to Ann Story Chapter of D. A. R. in Rutland.

GRAND ARMY OF THE REPUBLIC
WOMEN'S RELIEF CORPS

The Grand Army of the Republic was the organization of Civil War veterans; Kearney Post was listed in East Wallingford, but no other information about it was found. Kearney Women's Relief Corps met in Wallingford, in Greeno's Hall. It was, in a way, a G. A. R. auxiliary, although there were no requirements for membership except an interest in patriotic matters. The Corps realized an ambition of many years in 1931, when a monument in memory of the soldiers and sailors of the Civil, Spanish-American, and World Wars was placed in Green Hill Cemetery. It stands beside an older memorial, the urn which has on its base the inscription, "1861 To the Unknown Dead 1865."

The organization disbanded in 1932 after having had the responsibility since 1896 for the observance of Memorial Day, often called Decoration Day. On every May 30 for many years, children assembled at the school and marched to the cemetery, each carrying a bouquet of lilacs or lily-of-the-valley. After the bouquets had been dropped, one by one, beside the memorial urn, the line formed again to go to the cement bridge, where a small boat decorated with flowers was lowered gently to the water and allowed to sail down Otter Creek as a memorial to sailors. In South Wallingford, too, the children went "full school" to the Doty cemetery with their flowers. Later in the day "exercises" were held in the Town Hall, and the program included "pieces" spoken by the children; *Hats Off! the Flag is Passing By* was a favorite.

The observance of Memorial Day lost much of its poignancy with the passing of the last of the G. A. R. men. There is still a parade, but the celebration is much changed. After two world wars there are other veterans who are honored on Veterans' day, at a time of year when there are few flowers for the children to carry.

AMERICAN LEGION: Ralph H. Pickett Post No. 52

Chartered April 3, 1950, the Post was named for Ralph Pickett, a Wallingford boy and one of 400 Marines killed on Wake Island at the beginning of World War II. Others killed in action in that war were John Lambert, Raymond Livingston, Martin Reed, and Thomas Stack. Kenneth Weightman was killed in the Vietnam War.

There were 37 charter members, and the first commander was Major Robert A. Eddy, who served in both World Wars I and II. The Legion home on South Main Street, formerly George Sabin's Tin Shop, was given by the Town to the veterans of World War II.

In 1948, the Wallingford Color Guard headed the parade at the national convention of the Legion in New York City.

Each year the Legion sponsors a parade followed by a memorial service at the soldiers' monument in Green Hill Cemetery. Among the speakers at the Memorial Day services have been State Governors Dean Davis and Philip Hoff, and U. S. Senators George Aiken, Winston Prouty, and Robert Stafford.

Projects of the Legion include: Co-sponsor of Boy Scouts, Troop 12 (along with a group of interested citizens); contributions to the High School Band; sponsor of an oratorical contest among high school students on a patriotic subject; and provision, free of charge, of hospital equipment such as wheel chairs, crutches, and walkers, for use of people of Wallingford.

*   *   *   *

A Legion Auxiliary to Post No. 52 was formed on May 20, 1947, with 22 members, and Dorothy Bracken was elected President. Then on February 5, 1968, a new charter was approved by the National Secretary. There were then 12 charter members, with Mrs. Loretta Townsend, President.

The Auxiliary was awarded a Certificate of Appreciation and Recognition by the Vermont State Auxiliary for achievements during 1970 and 1971. It has contributed to many worthy causes including the Veterans' Hospital at White River Junction, the Old Soldiers' Home at Bennington, the Brandon Training School, and the Poppy Fund.

Gold Star Mothers: Mrs. Henry Howard, Mrs. Lambert, Mrs. Raymond Livingston, Mrs. Joseph Stack, and Mrs. Jenny Stenquist of Cuttingsville.

WALLINGFORD AMBULANCE COMPANY

The Wallingford Ambulance Company, No. 172 Vermont National Guard, was organized on December 10, 1921. There were about 45 members, and the commanding officers were Dr. Sherwin Cootey, Captain; Harry Townsend, 1st Lieutenant; John Seaver, 1st Sergeant; and Robert Eddy, 2nd Sergeant. The Company drilled regularly in the Town Hall, and attended National Guard Camp for a two week period each year. Among the camps attended were Fort Ethan Allen in Vermont, Camp Drum in New York, and state camps in Massachusetts, Connecticut, and Rhode Island. The unit at full strength had 20 ambulances, 2 trucks, 2 officers, and 55 men. The regular duties of the Company were transportation and first aid for the sick and wounded.

Fortunately, the Company was based here at the time of the flood in November, 1927. An article in the *Rutland Herald* reporting on the flood stated in part, "When the extent of the flood disaster was known in Wallingford, Dr. Cootey, acting as a reserve officer, at once took charge of matters and in a short time had ready for use 100 blankets, 1500 bushels of potatoes, a carload of meat which he commandeered in the railroad yard, as well as 1500 gallons of gasoline. Dr. Cootey ordered all gas stations to discontinue selling gas to anyone except farmers and trucks engaged in road work."

Following is an extract from Vermont National Guard records for the period ending June 20, 1928: "The officers of this organization, Captain Sherwin A. Cootey, Medical Corps, and Captain Harry B. Townsend, Medical Administrative Corps, Vermont National Guard, deserve special commendation for their persistence in maintaining the high standard morale and esprit, a superior type of enlisted personnel, training and condition, care and upkeep of transportation and equipment, which has been consistently maintained for three years." Apparently the original Ambulance Company was reorganized and redesignated during the period of that report, and became the 154th Ambulance Company, 118th Medical Regiment.

Then under the heading '1931 Inspection Reports' was this comment: "The 154th Ambulance Company should be commended for the fine spirit shown which is the result of conscientious training in spite of cramped quarters in the home armory. This company was awarded a cup for having the most sanitary area and kitchen. It is a fine organization."

By 1938 the Wallingford Ambulance Company had lost its identity and been absorbed by the 118th Medical Regiment. Included among the officers of that regiment were Sherwin A. Cootey, Rutland, Major, Medical Corps; Robert A. Eddy, Wallingford, Captain, Medical Administrative Corps, and Commanding Officer of Company F; and Levi C. Munson, Wallingford, Captain, Medical Administrative Corps.

CIVIL DEFENSE POLICE UNIT

This was a special police organization which met regularly for training, and took part in the nationwide air raid alerts of April, 1959, and May, 1960. Bert McClure was Chairman of the group, and Paul Mooney, Secretary. Other members were James Eisbrenner, Sherwin W. Fish, Raymond Guynup, Francis Hoadley, Harold Johnson, Ernest Lidstone, Ralph Lidstone, Selden Rapelye, Charles Rist, Howard Shaw, and Walter Wade. They also served the community by providing police patrols at Halloween, and for such special events as horse shows at Batcheller Field, and a sportsmen's show held at the Lake.

A First Aid course was sponsored, and in 1961, a Hunter Safety course for 51 Wallingford boys, girls, and adults. Organized and conducted by Sherwin W. Fish, National Rifle Association Safety Instructor, the course was held weekly for two months at the Wallingford Elementary and High Schools, with additional sessions for shooting instruction held in May in a field on upper Church Street. The course offered information regarding different types of guns, nomenclature of guns, gun handling, shooting, and safety practices. Also included were lessons in bow and arrow shooting, instructed by Ernest Lidstone. Upon completion of the course, the students received Hunter Safety certificates and shoulder patches.

Hunter Safety Instructors, certified by the Vermont Fish and Game Department, were Leo G. Benjamin and the members of the Police Unit.

WHITE ROCK FISH AND GAME CLUB

The club was active in the 1940's and 1950's; Tom Preedom was the first President. Among the projects sponsored were a fishing derby in Roaring Brook, and an early hunter safety course that included practice in the field. Some of the members got fingerling trout from the hatchery and kept them in the duckpond between Mill and Church Streets over the winter, fed them with food supplied by the hatchery, and then planted them in streams in the spring. Best remembered of the Club's activities were the game dinners, with venison, bear, and coon, served each fall in the Masonic Temple to enthusiastic crowds.

WHITE ROCK RIDERS, INC.

On February 2, 1972, a group of ardent snowmobilers met at the residence of Richard Kendall, Sr., for the purpose of organizing a club in which members could enjoy the companionship and recreation associated with the relatively new outdoor winter sport of snowmobiling. Officers were elected at the first meeting as follows: President, Dave Gilmore; Vice-President, Arthur Ingalls; Secretary-Treasurer, Mildred Marshall.

Membership grew rapidly and in December, 1972, the club was incorporated under the laws of the state of Vermont, and adopted the name of the White Rock Riders, Inc. The club also became a member of the Vermont Association of Snow Travelers (VAST) and adopted the code of ethics of VAST.

In addition to monthly meetings held during the winter months and various activities planned for the enjoyment of the club members, the club also participated in two county-wide ride-ins for the benefit of the Vermont Achievement Center. Several thousand dollars were raised for that very worthy organization. Also, an appreciation picnic was held in 1973 and again in 1974 to which all landowners were invited. This was a "thank you" to all those landowners who were kind enough to let the club put trails across their land. And, of course, at the end of each season a banquet has been held where all members can get together for an enjoyable evening.

There were 131 regular members and 12 junior members in the 1974-75 season. Officers for that season were: President, Dave Ballou; Vice-President, Ricky Baker; Secretary-Treasurer, Rolland Brown; Trailmaster, Fred Thurlow.

MASONS—Chipman Lodge No. 52, F. & A. M.
Mount Moriah Lodge No. 96, F. & A. M.

Chipman Lodge, chartered on January 11, 1861, was named after Supreme Court Judge Nathaniel Chipman. There were eleven charter members, and the first Master of the Lodge was Frederick Button, the Senior Warden, D. H. Sabin, and the Junior Warden, H. Shaw. Lodge meetings were held over George Sabin's Tin Shop.

In 1911 the Lodge purchased a two-story house on the north side of upper School Street. Around 1927-1928, the School Street property was sold and a house on South Main Street, near the original location, was purchased and has served since then as the Masonic Temple. An addition was built at the rear of the house to provide a large dining room on the first floor and a lodge room above.

The dining room, because of its large size and convenient kitchen facilities, has often been in demand and made available by the Lodge to outside organizations and individuals, for events such as strawberry festivals, chicken pie suppers, and wedding receptions. The membership of this lodge is now 93.

Mount Moriah Lodge is an outgrowth of Chipman Lodge of Wallingford. All of the founding fathers of Mount Moriah were members of Chipman Lodge. In their petition to the Grand Lodge of Vermont, asking to form a new Lodge, the distance over the mountain to Wallingford and the condition of the road were factors cited for the need of a new Lodge.

In 1870, the Grand Lodge permitted Chipman Lodge to hold alternate sessions at Wallingford and East Wallingford.

On June 26, 1871, Mount Moriah Lodge No. 96 received its charter from Grand Lodge. The first Master was Ransel Frost, the Senior Warden was Alvin Frost and the Junior Warden was Oscar Pelsue. Between 30 and 40 members constituted this early Lodge.

For four generations, Sewards have been active members and 5 of the living Sewards have served as Master. The present membership of this lodge is around 70.

The first Lodge rooms of the new Lodge were on the upper floor of the East Wallingford school. The present Lodge building was rented from Edwin and Mercy Chilson for several years. Around 1920 the building was purchased with the help of money willed the Lodge by Henry E. Goodell's daughter.

ORDER OF THE EASTERN STAR—Waverly Chapter No. 10

Waverly Chapter, then called Verde Mont, was first planned in May, 1874, and instituted in August of that year. One of its charter members, Mrs. Eliza G. Cole, was elected to the office of Worthy Grand Matron of the Grand Chapter of Vermont. However, in 1884 the chapter ceased to function. An entry in the old book reads: "Meeting opened in short form, not all officers present, no business to transact. The meeting closed."

The present chapter was rechartered on May 22, 1899, with the help of some of the first "Stars." Mrs. Phyllis Burditt was the first Worthy Matron after it was rechartered, serving again in that capacity in 1906 and 1907. It is interesting to note from the records that the brothers held the important offices and directed most of the ritualistic work, although the ladies were gaining more honorable mention.

The chapter has always been known for its work to help others. The Eastern Star Home and the Cancer Fund are its major projects. During various wartimes the chapter has contributed much in time and effort, such as knitting and bandage rolling.

The oldest member is Mrs. Ella Rogers, who celebrated her 103rd birthday March 18, 1975; she was active in the chapter into her nineties. She served as marshal for forty years, and then was elected marshal emeritus.

Waverly Chapter remembers with pride, among others, such names as: Mrs. Jessie Miller, Worthy Grand Matron, 1920; Dr. John Miller, Worthy Grand Patron, 1921, who worked unceasingly to make the O. E. S. Home a reality; Rev. Ola R. Houghton, Worthy Grand Patron, 1945-1946; and Mrs. Ella B. Seward, former charter member of Verde Monte who rejoined Waverly, Worthy Grand Matron, 1946-1947.

INDEPENDENT ORDER OF ODD FELLOWS
Pico Lodge No. 32
White Rock Rebekah Lodge No. 51

This Lodge was chartered August 23, 1871. The charter members were: Joel Todd, George W. Kinsman, E. O. Aldrich, Horace Todd, and Bradford Aldrich. The Lodge was instituted at Cuttingsville and removed to East Wallingford in July 1875.

The Wallingford Odd Fellows Association was formed on the 12th day of January, 1907. The first Directors were: President, Addison Stone; Vice-President, Frank Earle; Secretary, George Stafford; Treasurer, George Maxham.

Founded on the principles of "Love, Friendship and Truth" the association supports the Gill Home for the Aged in Ludlow, contributes to the eye bank so that others may see, and is active in many youth programs, for example, its Youth Camp in Maine for boys. More than 15,000 high school public speaking contest winners have received expense-free trips to the United Nations as guests of Odd Fellows and Rebekahs.

1975 officers are: Noble Grand, John Rist; Vice Grand, Warren Holland; Secretary, Frank Fox; Treasurer, Raymond Guynup.

The Wallingford Rebekah Lodge was instituted on August 29, 1902. A working team from Mechanicville, Vermont (now Belmont) was in Wallingford for the forming of the Lodge. There were also visitors present from Chester and Rutland. The first members were:

Mrs. Belle Parker	Mrs. Frank Earle
Mrs. L. H. Ellis	Mrs. W. C. Wood
Mrs. M. J. Clark	Mrs. S. J. Ainsworth
Mr. George M. Maxham	Mr. Frank L. Earle
Mrs. Asa J. Clemons	Mr. C. B. Wheeler
Mr. L. H. Ellis	Mr. S. J. Ainsworth

The oldest living members are: Edna Earle Shumway Maranville who joined in December 1915; Mary Edmunds in March 1918; and Ella Rogers in November 1920.

ROTARY INTERNATIONAL

The charter meeting of the Wallingford Rotary Club No. 2945, on July 25, 1928, was far more than the usual addition of another club to Rotary International. This remarkable organization was founded in Chicago, Illinois, February 5, 1905, by Paul P. Harris and friends. Because Founder Harris, having spent the impressionable years of boyhood in Wallingford, attested often to the influence of his paternal grandparents, Howard and Pamela Harris, Wallingford is known the world over as the birthplace of Rotary. He wrote, "Rotary was born of the spirit of tolerance, good will and service, all qualities that characterized New England folks of my boyhood days. . . ." The Rotary motto appropriately is "Service Above Self—He Profits Most Who Serves Best." Now, in 1975, there are 16,287 clubs with 768,250 members in 151 countries and geographical regions around the world; there are more countries in Rotary than there are in the United Nations.

For the chartering of the Wallingford Club in 1928, Paul Harris returned to his "New England Valley." He was the principal speaker at the dinner meeting, held in an ell of the Fork and Hoe Plant, and attended by more than 400 area Rotarians. The charter members were Dr. J. H. Miller, President, H. B. Barden, B. C. Batcheller, C. C. Cary, W. P. Cary, G. Crossland, C. A. Danolds, W. A. Davis, F. A. Dean, C. N. Foote, Rev. O. R. Houghton, M. J. B. Ingalls, T. V. Kirk, N. G. Miller, R. C. Taft, P. W. Thayer, and H. B. Townsend. Regular meetings of the Club were held first in the Congregational Church, and then at True Temper Inn. Average membership over the years has been 32.

In 1928, six Rutland Rotarians who were boyhood friends of Paul Harris, formed a corporation and purchased the small red brick schoolhouse on Main Street where Paul had learned his A, B, C's. This building was erected in 1818 by James Rustin, great-grandfather of Paul. It has been used variously as a school, chapel, health center, Red Cross workroom, residence, and tea room. The Corporation gave the stewardship of the building to the Wallingford Club in 1948, and since then it has met there regularly on Mondays at 6:30 P.M. In 1962 the property was turned over to the Club, which is now the sole owner. Soon after, the fifty-year old kitchen ell was replaced by a new, modern kitchen, with much of the construction being done by the members.

This Rotary shrine has made Wallingford known internationally. Each year Rotarian Governor-Nominees from around the world attend a special meeting for them in the building. More than 500 clubs have presented their banners, which decorate the hall. Also displayed are Paul Harris memorabilia, including many items presented to him during his trips around the world.

Rotary Building. Lithograph by Ella Fillmore Lille

In addition to Rotarian activities, the building is made available rent free, often several times a week, for community meetings such as Scouts, Green Hill Homemakers, school and town planning committees, and others. Two major fund-raising projects each year which help to provide for the upkeep of the property are the Rotary Play and the Rotary Auction.

Rotary's most recent service project is the conducting of a Hunter Safety Course; such a course is now required by law before a would-be hunter can get his first hunting license. The course includes 10 hours of instruction, use of a text-book and movies, and a practice session out-of-doors. It was given twice this year (1975) and 27 persons, ranging in age from 8 to 35, were graduated. Instructors were three Rotarians, David Ballou, Lee Lawson, and Edward Patch, who have all taken a training course at Castleton, and two guest instructors, a game warden and a doctor.

The Paul P. Harris Memorial Building is now listed as a Vermont Historical Site and a marker so indicating stands in front of the property. It was dedicated in 1966 by Rotarian Philip H. Hoff, then Governor of the State of Vermont.

Chapter 7

Schools and Libraries

SCHOOLS

From the earliest years Wallingford Township was divided into school districts, and by 1869 there were 14 with a schoolhouse in each. The schools were named according to their location—Centerville, West Hill, South Wallingford—or for a neighboring family—Munson, Sweetland, Hemenway. By 1897 the Town Report shows that the number of schools had been reduced to seven. In the six rural schools there were from 9 to 38 pupils; at Wallingford village there were 139, with a total for all the schools of 258. In these seven schools "All the Blackboards are wood except one stone one in the Sweetland school building. All are so located, in relation to windows, as to receive light from each side and in front. All the school grounds are provided with the necessary outbuildings. There is no plumbing in any of the school buildings except the High School building and this is in good condition."

The first school building in Wallingford village was the present Rotary Building, and there were also various "select" or private schools. The building on School Street, known at first as the North School, later as the High School, was built in 1865 and graded throughout in 1871. According to the Superintendent's report in March, 1909, an addition to this building had been made, the lower room was finished and had been used for the high school classes during the preceding year. The upper room was not finished until later, although the Superintendent fitted up a temporary office in one corner.

At a special meeting in 1910, a proposition to have a first class high school was voted down. The village building remained the same through 1911 except that one room had been "ceiled up" for high school use. Minor improvements had been made to freshen up the rooms with paint "at a small cost." However, sanitary and safety conditions were neglected, and on July 1, 1912, the school was condemned by the State Board of Health. That fall, classes were conducted in the Congregational Chapel and the Town Hall, and work was started on the renovations to the village building. At the town meeting in 1914, school was dismissed for the day so that all could inspect the renovations, which included flush toilets throughout and a fire escape to the south of the building. After noting that the State Health officer had recommended some of these improvements as early as 1906, Dr. J. H. Miller, a long-time school director, commented, "Good things come slowly."

Centerville School, 1898. L. to R., back row: Alice Armstrong, teacher; Drusilla Kent, Maude Rounds, Maggie Bourne, Mary Barber, Lydia White, Elzina Pelsue, Lizzie Mulqueen. Second row, Johnny Pelsue, his brother, Hosea Pelsue, Wyatt Kent, Eddie Mulqueen, Willie Rounds. Third row, Little Miss Barber, Lydia Barber, Mary Pelsue, Johnnie Bourne, Agnes Bourne, Mary Stewart.

The elementary grades for Wallingford village, and high school classes for the town, were housed in this building for many years, with improvements being made whenever possible. In 1928, after an oil burner had been installed, a science laboratory was built and fitted in an area in the basement formerly used for coal storage. Enrollments continued to increase and more classroom space was needed; some classes were being held in the Town Hall. In 1934, work was completed on an addition on the west side of the building, which included a gymnasium and two new classrooms. The gymnasium was made possible by the generosity of Mr. Birney C. Batcheller; it was dedicated at the graduation ceremonies in 1935.

Until the gymnasium was built, basketball games were played in the old True Temper Inn garage which accommodated only a few spectators. The new gym provided much more seating capacity and was welcomed enthusiastically by parents and friends. Accordingly there was great disappointment when it no longer met established standards and was outlawed for interscholastic competition in the 1960's. However, it still served a number of useful purposes.

One day in 1942, the oil burner exploded causing $400 damage two hours before time for school. Plaster fell and windows were blown out and the whole school was covered with black soot. There was no fire after the explosion, and as it happened so early in the morning no one was in the school and there were no injuries. The room which had the most damage, including fallen plaster, housed children of grades one and two, so there was much to be thankful for. Many of the older boys and girls pitched in to help clean up, even if it did mean that the school bell would ring again all the sooner.

The school population continued to grow, and in the 40's some elementary classes were once more housed in the Town Hall, and in the Masonic Temple. In 1952 a new elementary building was constructed in back of the old school. It contained five grade rooms, a multi-purpose room, a kitchen, a health room, a conference room, and a teachers' work room. There were 141 pupils. In 1969 an addition was made to this building, providing more class rooms to accommodate two sections for each grade, thereby lowering the teacher-pupil ratio for a better education. Also included were a kindergarten room with its own entrance, a gymnasium/auditorium with a stage, a larger kitchen, and storage rooms. The former multi-purpose room was converted to a library, which for a time was used by both the elementary grades and the high school.

Wallingford Elementary School

For many years there were nine grades, and graduation exercises were held at the Town Hall for those who finished. Few went on to the High School, which offered only a two year college preparatory course; a three year course had been tried but found not satisfactory. In 1897 German was added to the course so that students could have the subjects necessary for entrance to college. In 1906 and 1908, some students completed two years in Wallingford High School and then went directly to institutions of higher learning.

Around 1915 the Grammar School was changed from nine grades to eight, and a commercial preparatory course was offered in the High School. Enrollment increased; six boys and nine girls elected the commercial course, while one boy and two girls followed the college course, a total of 18. In the next two years enrollment increased to 42 in the High School. Those following the commercial course usually found jobs at the completion of two years' study or went on to business schools before being employed. In 1918, Eveline Houghton completed four years of High School and became the first four-year graduate and the only one in her class. Since that time there have been four-year graduates every year—small classes at first and in later years over forty.

Commencement exercises for the early four year graduates were combined with the customary exercises for those finishing Grammar School. In 1920 this practice was changed, and exercises held only for those finishing High School. It was about this same time that the term Junior High School began to be used for the 7th and 8th grades. One reason for both of these changes was to encourage students to continue on to High School and not think that the 8th grade was a good stopping place.

By the 1920's there were more than a hundred students in the Junior-Senior High School, enrolled in either a standard or a college-preparatory course. Two years of French and four of Latin were offered instead of German. Commercial courses had been discontinued, but agriculture and home economics were being taught, and for a time a special shop course was conducted with the cooperation of the American Fork and Hoe Company. The boys worked at some trade at the shop under the guidance of shop personnel and had their academic work at school; this was discontinued in the 1930's.

Later, shop courses were taught at the school, at first in the basement of the school, and then the building which had been Harry Townsend's garage was rented and renovated for shop work. Juniors and seniors had a four period course at this location until Rutland High School offered vocational courses to students from outlying towns. After that, the building was used for shop courses for grades 7-10, and the upper classmen were transported to Rutland. Commercial classes were added gradually. At first they were carried on in the senior hall with a part time teacher, then as an integral part of the school program with a full time commercial teacher.

Programs and services for both elementary and high school students have been improved and enlarged over the years. The first public kindergarten in the town opened in the fall of 1967. By that time the school bus was a familiar sight, and transportation for students living too far from the school to walk was taken for granted. This represented a big change from the early years, when students entering high school from the rural schools found their own transportation or lived with families in the village, sometimes working for their board and room.

The Federal Hot Lunch project began in 1945, when the Home Economics Department began serving a meal just during the winter months. One hot dish, dark bread, fruit, and milk were served for 10c or the equivalent in commodities. The 1953 Town Report noted that a more satisfactory program could be offered in the new elementary school building. Hot lunches continue to be served, all during the school year, and the regular price now is 35¢.

The elementary school library, and the combined high school and town library, were important additions to the reading program and re-

High School Band, 1932. L. to R. standing, Thomas Stack, Eugene LaFrancis, Paul Taft, Hugh Stack, Eunice Bugbee, Elbert Cole, John Miller. Seated, Elwin Parker, Stearns Hatch, Albert Bulley, Philip Cary, Ann Benson, Robert McClure, Oville Boule.

sources for all branches of the curriculum. Just recently, a special reading teacher has been added to the elementary staff, to work with youngsters whose reading is below their grade level. The use of audio-visual aids has increased in all areas, and more field trips are taken. Health checkups have been arranged and subsidized through a P. T. A. committee. Physical Education has been available to all students, in addition to regular sports activities including, in recent years, skiing. Driver training was offered in the High School from 1948 on.

Art, and arts and crafts programs, have been added from time to time. Music, including instruction, band, and choirs, has become an important part of the curriculum, with a full-time teacher; parent groups subsidized the early years with part-time vocal and instrumental teachers, and bought uniforms and some instruments. In 1971, Mrs. Kenneth Anderson became the music instructor; she was particularly successful with the band. Almost 100 high school and elementary students participated, and the band took part in a number of parades.

Although Wallingford has been one of the small schools in the state, with limited facilities and curriculum offerings, its students have been able to compete successfully with those of larger schools. They had one state championship in Debate, and twice were entered in the New England finals in Drama; competition in these areas is among all schools in the state regardless of size. Then, in Class C or M competition,

High School Band, 1975. Memorial Day Parade

W. H. S. was state champion in basketball five times and in baseball once.

Over the years students have continued their education and graduated from various colleges, including the University of Vermont, Harvard, M. I. T., Middlebury, the Air Force Academy, and Dartmouth. Others have received degrees in nursing from U. V. M., Mary Hitchcock Hospital in Hanover, the Deaconess Hospital in Boston, and others. Still other alumni have graduated from state colleges, technical schools, business colleges, and various special schools.

Wallingford had the first high school weekly newspaper in the state, which provided a link between the school, the townspeople, and the alumni. Some of the news articles were contributed by elementary students from the village school, and from the rural schools while they were in existence.

The early school districts were largely self-governing, although town records indicate that school matters were often referred to the selectmen, for instance if a family wished to be "set off" from one district to another. After 1853, a superintendent for all schools was appointed by a committee elected at town meeting. With a change in the state law in 1892, the districts lost their autonomy and all school matters were governed by the town School Board, including the appointment of the superintendent. In 1908, Wallingford joined with the towns of Clarendon, Middletown Springs, Shrewsbury, and Tinmouth to form a supervisory district, of which Carroll H. Drown was the first superintendent. Except for a time in the 20's and 30's when there was a supervising principal for all the Wallingford schools, the town has continued in one or another supervisory union.

When the number of school districts was large, it was impossible for the superintendent to cover them adequately. For many years, consolidation was urged, and the number of districts decreased gradually. In 1967, the last step to consolidation was taken when the East Wallingford school was closed and its pupils too were transported to the elementary school in Wallingford village.

For almost 30 years there was study and consultation on the formation of a union high school district, and several votes were taken. All of these were supported in Wallingford but defeated in one of the other towns involved. Finally, in 1974, Clarendon, Shrewsbury, and Wallingford voted to form Union 40, and to build a high school for those three towns. The school, built in Clarendon and named the Mill River Union High School, opened in September of 1975 for students of grades 7-12. Demolition of the old Wallingford High School started June 14, 1975, and the Alma Mater of many Wallingford students is no more.

In that year (1975), the three towns withdrew from their supervisory districts, and Rutland South Supervisory Union was formed, comprising

Clarendon, Shrewsbury, Wallingford, and Union 40. The first super-intendent is Henry Burnham, a Wallingford native and a graduate of Wallingford High School.

Now, in 1975, the Wallingford educational system has completed a cycle in its history. Fourteen single schools have been gradually con-solidated into one, housed in a modern, well-equipped building, with a full-time principal. The programs at the elementary school and the new union high school are under the direction of the same superintendent. Responsibility for the entire school program is entrusted by citizens and parents to elected School Board members.

GILBERT HART LIBRARY

As it stands there on Main Street, the Library looks from the front just as it did in the fall of 1910. The room to the south, planned as a children's room, had been added that summer. The windows were set high in the walls, to leave space below for "maps, pictures, etc., that would instruct and attract the children," as Mr. Hart wrote in 1909. He had given the original Library in 1894, and now he wanted to provide a

Drawing of Gilbert Hart Library, by Natalie MacIntyre

larger and better room for the children of the town. He went on to say that poor children especially appealed to him, because he never could forget the privations that existed when he was a poor boy living in Hartsboro seventy years before.

Mrs. Martha Edgerton remembered bringing her pupils from South Wallingford to the dedication of the new room. The children wanted to come, but had no transportation and thought the walk both ways too long. They were delighted when the use of a wagon with a hay rack was offered, and they were able to make the trip. Children from a number of other schools also came, to hear stories told. When Mrs. Ned J. Scribner called attention to the splendid gift that had come to children through Mr. Hart's generosity and asked for three cheers for him, they were given with a will.

The children's room was the first in a series of changes. The next, in 1940, was the addition at the back of the building, which almost doubled it in size and included a basement room with a 2-story stack room above. Only part of this stack room has ever been used; a temporary ceiling cuts off the upper part, which could be put into service should more shelf space be needed. When the books had been moved into the new stack room, the old stack room, which still housed the librarian's desk, became the children's room. The former children's room, now somewhat

The Library, north side view

isolated, was used for the increasing store of material related to Vermont and to Wallingford. The reading room continues in the same use, but it has more shelves and bookcases than in the old days, the Civil War memorial has been moved to the hall, and the great oak table that filled the center of the room has been sold. A minor remodelling in 1969 moved the librarian's desk to a more convenient central location. The most recent improvements to the building, in 1973, involved safety measures: a fire escape, fire walls in the furnace room, and changing the front doors to open outward.

The 1973 improvements permitted the High School library, crowded for space, to be moved out of the elementary library and merged temporarily with the town library, until the students moved to the new union school. The Library and the schools have always worked well together; early librarians' reports note special loans of books to students, and at times library hours have been lengthened during the school year. Now that the Elementary School has its own library, an effort is made to have materials in the Library supplement rather than duplicate those at school, and the two collections are catalogued in the same way so that students can use both easily.

To accept for the people of Wallingford Mr. Hart's gift of the Library, the Gilbert Hart Library Association was organized in 1893 and chartered by the State in 1894. It has continued to maintain and operate the Library through its Board of Trustees. The members elect three Trustees each year to serve for a term of three years, and the officers are elected from among the Trustees. In the early years, membership was by invitation. A member was voted in, signed the By-Laws, and paid $1 for a life membership. Now everyone is solicited, even urged, to join the Association; dues for a family are $1 a year, which is used to buy new books.

Support for the Library in its first year was from voluntary subscriptions and the membership dues. Beginning in 1895, tax money has been voted, at first from the Town, so many cents on the grand list, and since 1964 as an item in the school budget. This tax money has been supplemented by individual contributions of money, goods, and services. In the earliest By-Laws was a stipulation that members would pay any assessment voted at any regular meeting. An undated letter from the Clerk regarding one such assessment asked that members "please be good about it and pay this small sum (50¢) promptly and cheerfully."

A Book of Remembrance and old records kept at the Library list bequests and sums given in trust or as memorials; income from these funds amounts to $200 or $300 a year, and is used for books or whatever purpose was designated. The Avery Dean Fund, for instance, was given by Mr. and Mrs. F. A. Dean after their son died as a very young man;

it was money Avery had earned working at True Temper Inn while he was in High School; the income is used for children's books. Many of the books on the shelves are gifts, some carrying a plate that says they are in memory of a neighbor, friend, or relative. And there have been all sorts of fund-raising projects—book sales, food sales, lawn parties, a card party, a minstrel show that had three performances in the 1920's; in the 1950's, the Summer Festival helped.

Old records also list the names of many, natives and newcomers, who have served the Association and the Library. W. C. Mason, manager of the Batcheller Works and Mr. Hart's correspondent on Library matters, was the first President. Birney C. Batcheller was a long-time President; it was he who gave the 1940 addition as well as the pictures that hang in the Vermont Room. During those same years, Miss Mary Howley was Treasurer, and Miss Marion Tryon was Auditor. In the early 1960's, Miss Tryon donated her services almost full time for many months while the books were being catalogued. Mrs. Mary Gilbert Smith acted as Treasurer, as the Secretary who wrote the liveliest minutes, and as chairman of a number of fund-raising projects; sometimes at lawn parties she dressed in gypsy costume and told fortunes. Dr. and Mrs. Kingman founded the Pay Shelf, which added books to the Library for forty years. John Hoadley was President, and made the magazine rack; his family gave the record player. Library notepaper has a drawing of the building done by Natalie MacIntyre. Natalie Congdon was recently President for a number of terms. Officers elected in October, 1975, were Wendell Weeks, President; Amy Bouley, Vice-President; Sandra Marquis, Secretary; Ernest Downie, Treasurer.

The original book collection consisted of 1000 volumes recommended to Mr. Hart by a Detroit librarian, and some other gift books. The number has grown gradually and steadily to about 11,500 now. More books are also available through interlibrary loan, and in collections borrowed from the Regional Library. Figures on use of the books show that circulation was highest in the 1930's, declined after that, and has again been increasing in recent years. About half of the books continue to be fiction; as for the rest, travel and philosophy are less in demand than formerly, while more science, handicraft, and do-it-yourself books are on the shelves. Of course the wealth of handsome children's books was just not available early in the century. Recordings are a recent addition, and films can be obtained for groups which request them.

During the early years, books were chosen by a committee. Its members apparently took suggestions from Association members and then bought from Rutland bookshops the books which they had read and approved for the Library. That custom could not survive the tremendous increase in the number of books being published. First the librarian, who had access to reviews, lists, and professional recommendations, and also knew first-hand what books were in demand, was made a member of the committee. Finally the committee disappeared entirely. It is now Library policy that the librarian is responsible for the selection of all library material in the Library.

Prior to the opening of the Library in 1894, the trustees invited applications for the position of librarian, and two were received. Unable to decide between the two applicants, the trustees asked for bids for the year's work. One bid was for $200, but the place was given to Miss Jennie Ferry, who bid $184 "to take charge of the building." She stayed only one year, and was followed by Miss Minnie Townsend, 1895-1896, Miss May L. Congdon, 1896-1920, Mrs. Iva Hawkins, 1920-1942, Mrs. Anna Crossland, 1942-1960, and since 1960, Mrs. Anna H. Hoadley. There were for a long time small branch libraries in homes in East and South Wallingford; both were discontinued about the time that the State began sending Bookmobiles out. These, too, are now a thing of the past, and the State is experimenting with a book-by-mail service to individuals.

During the first years of the Library, the reading-room was much more used than now, in fact, only that part of the Library was open on Sunday afternoons. In 1924 it was voted that the magazines on the reading table should be put into circulation, something very few libraries do. In 1949, the subscriptions to metropolitan newspapers were discontinued because the librarian reported that they were little used, and the money was spent for more magazines. People still come to the Library to read, but it is less likely to be for recreation than a search for specific information in reference books, or in the Library's generous store of Vermontiana and local history. One such item is the record book of the first library in Wallingford, so early that its accounts were kept in English money.

Other uses of the Library property have been made from time to time. Years ago there was a tennis court in the back yard, enjoyed especially by the local clergy. Band concerts used to be held on the front lawn. A meeting place for a short-lived Historical Society was provided. Civil defense supplies were stored in the basement. Student art has been displayed. All in all, the Library has been and continues to be important in the life of the community.

Chapter 8

Churches and Cemeteries

THE CHURCHES

The building of the first church in the town was discussed at Town Meeting in 1795. It was erected a mile south of Wallingford village, occupied by 1800, and paid for with tax money. Used as a Union Meeting House up to the time the Baptist Church was built, it then became the Town House, where for a few years Town Meetings were held. There was also a Union Meeting House on Sugar Hill, near the cemetery, which was in use for about 30 years between 1830 and 1860.

There has been other activity involving cooperation among the different denominations. In 1958 a group of parents from all three churches in Wallingford village, brought together by Father Connor, formed an organization called Parents Together. For three successive years the group sponsored a series of forums each spring on the problems of bringing up children. Clergy from the three churches formed an advisory committee, and young people from the community were included in the programs.

In the spring of 1975, as a result of the spontaneous interest and working together that sometimes occurs, an ecumenical dinner was held at the Masonic Temple. Sister Elizabeth Candon, President of Trinity College in Burlington, spoke to a considerable number of women from the various churches. Then on Christmas Sunday of 1975, a cantata was presented at the Congregational Church, with members from all three of the village churches taking part, working on committees, and singing in the choir.

FIRST BAPTIST CHURCH, WALLINGFORD

The Baptist Church of Wallingford is the oldest church in Wallingford township, and also the oldest Baptist church in Vermont. It was organized on February 10, 1780, as the First Church of Wallingford, but soon after became the Baptist Church because the "prevailing sentiment" among the organizers was Baptist. Meetings were held at the residences of members until 1800, and then at the Union Meeting House.

In 1827 the First Baptist Church building was erected at a cost of $870. It was repaired in 1869 at a cost of $2000. The building was again repaired in 1904, and a chapel and several small rooms were added. In 1921, the Church acquired the parsonage by a gift from the Trustees who had owned it.

Baptist Church, Wallingford

Membership and attendance have fluctuated widely. Membership reached its peak of 225 in 1805, when 114 were received into the Church following a revival the previous year. In 1894, the church minutes of October 29 stated, "Only 8 present tonight," and on November 29, "Thanksgiving day, and at church and prayer meeting this evening there were present 18. A good spirit. No business." In 1923, there were 118 members, including 86 in residence. The average attendance in Sunday School then was 42.

At various times during its long life the Church has needed financial assistance, and has received it, in part, from the Vermont Baptist State Convention.

During the Reverend Aubert's first pastorate, 1912-17, the Church adopted "the New Testament standard of church finances. The policy of buying was changed to the method of giving." It was stated that "the experiences of this Church in the matter of giving prove that suppers, fairs, bazaars, and all things of like character are not necessary to the Church which honors her Lord in stewardship." During the second Aubert pastorate, "The emphasis has been placed upon the power of prayer rather than upon the efficacy of methods to produce spiritual results."

A weekly radio broadcast "Ambassadors for Christ" was started in 1948 by the Reverend Westerholm, and continued for nineteen years over Rutland Radio Station WSYB.

In 1950, the average attendance at Sunday School was 70. Then for a six week period, during the "Christian Life Contest," starting March, 1951, an alltime high of 110 was reached. But whether Sunday School attendance was large or small, a Bible-teaching ministry has always been provided for boys and girls in the community.

Again quoting from Mrs. Aubert's Sketch of the First Baptist Church (1930), "In spite of limited membership, limited means, brief pastorates, the ministry of this church has continued for 150 (now 195) years, and God alone can declare the results."

Pastors who have served the Baptist Church, 1910 to 1976

S. David Sikes	1910-1911	Dexter D. Emery	1943-1945
Howard B. Smith	1911-1912	Frank M. Beach	1946-1947
Adolph Aubert	1912-1917	Walter Westerholm	1948-1952
J. S. Stowell	1917-1918	Charles E. Davis	1953-1955
W. C. Goodwin	1918-1921	H. Bruce Stone	1956-1964
Dirk Van de Voet	1921-1924	Richard Sutter	1964-1974
J. S. Brown	1924-1927	Richard Seitler	1974-
Adolph Aubert	1927-1942		

FIRST CONGREGATIONAL CHURCH, WALLINGFORD

Early church records have been lost, but town records indicate that the Congregational Church and Society were organized between 1787 and 1793. The Society was the business and legal instrument of the Church; in 1917, Articles of Association were signed and filed in the office of the Secretary of State of Vermont, and the Church became one entity, First Congregational Church. In 1960, this Church and others of the denomination voted to join the United Church of Christ, formed by a merger of Congregational and Reformed churches.

Church services were held first in homes, at the Union Meeting House until 1827, and then at the Baptist Church until 1829, when the present Congregational Church building was completed. Soon after, a bell was purchased to be "rung at all meetings of the Church and Society and tolled whenever necessary." In 1831, the Society appointed a committee to raise money to finish off the basement "in whole or in part." This was finally done 91 years later, when it was "finished off in whole" under the direction of architect Paul Thayer in 1922. In the meantime, new pews were added, electric lights installed, and stained glass windows put in. In 1863 the former school house was acquired; it was commonly called the Chapel and was used for small group meetings until the basement rooms in the church building became available, when it was sold to Rotary.

Congregational Church, Wallingford

Extensive repairs had to be made to the church following a fire in 1954. At that time the new pulpit was built at the side of the platform, balanced by a lectern on the other, and with the Communion table at the central position formerly occupied by the pulpit.

An 1834 bequest to the Church was designated for support of the Sunday School, which has continued to be an important and basic activity. Classes for children and young people through high school age have been held on Sunday morning for as long as anyone can remember. From time to time there have been special programs for young people. During Mr. Houghton's pastorate, the Christian Endeavor Society held discussion type meetings on Sunday evenings in the chapel. The Pilgrim Fellowship was active in the 1950's and '60's, and its members were largely responsible for the installation of the chimes.

After the Civil War, Miss Eliza Huntoon went from the Church as a teacher in one of the schools established in the South by Home Mission Boards for the freed slaves; she was later Superintendent of Schools here in Wallingford. Around the turn of the century three young men from the Church entered the ministry, Henry L. Ballou, William J. Ballou, and Frank J. Scribner. George Greenough, who had finished his theological studies while teaching in the local high school, was ordained in the Church April 22, 1951; he is now pastor of a church in Whitehall, New York.

In 1894 the envelope system of missionary giving was adopted, and still continues. "One Great Hour of Sharing" and other special benevolence offerings are taken each year. The Women's Fellowship, dedicated to the benevolent work of the Church, has its own projects such as the layettes and health kits made in 1975, and the 800 pounds of new and used clothing packed for Church World Service.

All women of the Church are automatically members of the Fellowship, and also of the Ladies Aid Society, which was organized in 1883 "to do benevolent work for the needy of the community and second, to raise money to assist in carrying on the work of the Congregational Church in Wallingford." Two of its projects have become traditional, the May Breakfast and the Midsummer Country Fair. The financial rewards from these projects are welcome, but the emphasis is on the giving of service, the using of talents, and working together. The Fortnightly, organized in 1893, is a smaller group which has a program designed to carry out the original purpose of the Society, "to promote the intellectual, cultural, and social life of its members."

Pastors who have served the Congregational Church since 1910:

Walter Thorpe	1906-1915	George P. Weiss	1953-1963
Ola R. Houghton	1915-1948	Richard P. Armstrong	1964-
William M. Edwards	1948-1953		

Ola R. Houghton was elected Pastor Emeritus on his retirement in 1948. George Paul was Supply Pastor for several months during the illness of Rev. Weiss.

UNION CONGREGATIONAL CHURCH, SOUTH WALLINGFORD

This church was built in the summer of 1840 under the direction of nineteen year old Albert Mathewson, with lumber cut from nearby trees, and on land donated by Holden Stafford. Also some fine pine boards, brought from northern New York, were used in the building. Many townspeople worked on it. One man helping with the building of the church was in a great hurry to get the roof on. When asked why, he

Union Congregational Church, South Wallingford

said it should be done as soon as possible "to keep the devil without and the Spirit within." Money for the building was obtained from some seventy subscribers. The church's facade remains the same today as when it was built.

On November 3, 1896, an organization and dedication service was held, with Reverend Tupper as Chairman; Miss Abbie Chapin was named Clerk. The first pastor, and the only one to settle in South Wallingford, was Reverend Dennis Chapin, a Universalist. The membership in those days was about 24.

During intervening years the pulpit was supplied in the summers by young men from Theological Seminaries. Then from about 1905 on, services have been held the year around by the pastor of the Congregational Church in Wallingford.

Life centered around and in this Church. A Christian Endeavor Society met on Sunday evenings, and raised funds for the Church by hard work and fun. Cantatas and other musical programs were presented under the direction of Mr. Linwood Taft, a teacher who gave the Church a pipe organ, and encouraged an appreciation for dramatic, literary, and musical programs.

The Ladies Aid was formed in November, 1894. The first meetings were held in homes where "most enjoyable" five o'clock teas were served. In November, 1910, the Ladies Aid accepted an offer by Mr. Frank Earl to hold their meetings in a room over his blacksmith shop. Now (1975) meetings are held in the church basement or at the nearby Youth Center.

The Ladies Aid has always been an enterprising and energetic group of ladies, and has raised money for repairs to the church and in support of church activities. For example, back in 1899 they contributed funds to build horse sheds behind the church, to protect horse and wagon from the weather during church services. These sheds, when gaily decorated, served as booths for display of items for sale at Bazaars and other fund-raising projects of the Ladies Aid.

EAST WALLINGFORD BAPTIST CHURCH

May 17, 1859 was the day of adoption of the By-Laws of the East Wallingford Meetinghouse Association. Twenty-seven members of the community were the original signers. Officers elected June 29, 1859, were: President, O. L. Allen; Secretary-Treasurer, A. Constantine; Trustees, Loomis French, P. B. Lincoln, and Tomas York; Collector, P. R. Fuller. Throughout the fall of 1859 and spring of 1860 many people contributed various sums of money, bought an Association share, or purchased a pew. Jacob Gray was hired to construct the meeting-house, and September, 1860, saw the completion of the project.

The spiritual needs of the people were met very well for about twenty years, before disinterest set in. By 1885 there were not enough people to hold business meetings; sometimes no one showed up for a meeting. But soon interest was renewed. The church was repainted and refurbished in 1892, and in 1894 a new bell acquired. A Ladies Aid Society was formed in 1904. In 1905, the name "Meetinghouse Association" was changed to "Church," and the church was incorporated according to state laws. A Christian Endeavor Society was formed the next year, and in 1909 a baptistry was installed. Later, the construction of a vestry on the back of the church provided a kitchen, dining room, and upstairs classroom.

On August 20, 1935, two anniversary parties were held at the church. One anniversary celebrated 106 years of Bible teaching in East Walling-ford, and the other, the seventy-fifth anniversary of the church. In 1941,

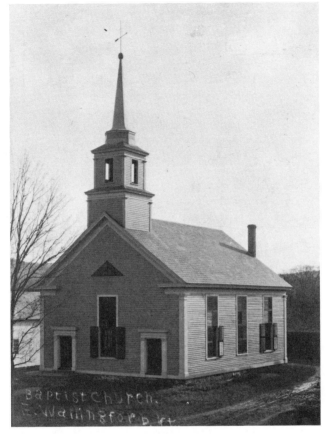

Baptist Church, East Wallingford

the Sunday School of Sugar Hill, run by the Jennings family, and the East Wallingford Sunday School were merged, and twenty-five people from the two Sunday Schools were baptized. Daily Vacation Bible School was started in 1945, to reach young children of the village. By 1950, fifty-five children were attending each summer. In 1961, a talk by Paul Bubar from Word of Life in Schroon Lake, New York, prompted the formation of a Word of Life Club.

During 1968, Pastor Flatt and Carl Kavanaugh completely remodelled the upstairs room in the vestry, and major repairs have also been made at the parsonage in recent years. The repair on the buildings has been matched by spiritual repairs. More missionaries are now supported, a youth group started by Word of Life Bible Institute students is very active, prayer meeting is an important part of weekly services, and special meetings emphasize the Lord's work.

Pastors who have served the Baptist Church since 1910:

Frederick Emerson	1910-1912	C. L. Osterhout	
F. W. Buck	1912-1915	F. B. Boone	
			1926-1929
George W. Russell		T. Ford Barker	
	1915-1919		
William J. Millet		H. P. Weatherbee	
Edgar Johnson	1919-1926		
H. Campbell Eatough	1929-1930	Student Pastor	
George E. Millard	1930-1931	Student Pastor	

From 1931 to 1952, the pastors from the Wallingford and Ludlow Baptist Churches served the East Wallingford Church.

Claude C. Berry	1952-1961	David Daniels	1971-1972
Vern Haskell	1961-1965	Claude C. Berry	1972-1975
R. Robert Flatt	1966-1970	A. Douglas Ferry	1975-

ST. PATRICK'S ROMAN CATHOLIC CHURCH, WALLINGFORD

St. Patrick's Church was built during 1865 and 1866 from stone quarried nearby. Men of the church helped with the construction, some of them coming after work at the shop. In 1911 a rectory was built south of the church.

The interior of the church was first remodeled and redecorated under the direction of Father Hackett. Then in 1972, other changes were made to conform with diocesan and papal requirements. Money left to the church by the will of Katie McConnell was used in 1935 to rebuild the Marble Altar. The statue of the Virgin Mary was donated by Florence Dawson Whalen in memory of her mother, Mary Dawson Ladabouche.

In May, 1954, the outdoor Shrine to our Lady of Knock was dedicated by Bishop Ryan. This was the first outside shrine of its kind to be constructed in this country. The original Shrine is located in Knock, Ireland.

The building north of the church was purchased sometime in the 1950's and converted into a "Parish Center." During Father Fitzpatrick's time a sizeable addition to the building was completed. This parish center is used for various youth group and Rosary Alter Society meetings. It is being paid for by donations, and with funds raised by the Altar Society through food sales and the annual Christmas Bazaar.

The Rosary Altar Society was formed in 1957 and was originally for members only. Now it is open to all women of the parish and many help with the various Society projects. The present membership is approximately 100.

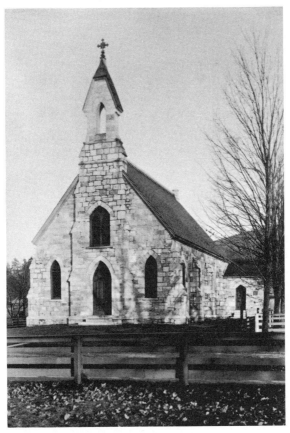

Catholic Church, Wallingford

Religious education at St. Patrick's starts with children in the first grade and continues with them through adulthood. Children in the three primary grades are taught by those women in the parish who have taken courses given by a religious education coordinator. Fourth, fifth, and sixth graders traditionally had catechism once a week after school, but recently have had longer sessions in the morning during vacation periods. Young adults in the higher grades, along with their parents, attend sessions taught by the pastor and the religious education coordinator.

The membership of St. Patrick's is now approximately 500, and of St. Mary's Mission in Mt. Holly around 360. Masses are celebrated at St. Patrick's at 5:30 P.M. on Saturday, and at 8 and 11 A.M. on Sunday. Also there is a Sunday Mass at St. Mary's Mission. On other days of the week, a morning or evening Mass is celebrated at St. Patrick's.

Priests who have served St. Patrick's Parish since 1910:

T. O'Donoghue	1910-1911	T. H. Connor*	1944-1960
Thomas Henry	1911-1915	J. P. Ryan	1960-1963
Arthur Griffin	1915-1924	R. M. Cronan	1963-1965
J. A. Thompson	1924-1930	C. E. Fitzpatrick	1955-1971
J. H. McCarthy	1930-1937	R. D. Walsh	1971-1976
W. P. Hackett	1937-1944	Donald Ritchie	1976-

*On March 22, 1970, Father Connor received the honorary title of Monsignor for his many years of devoted service in the Diocese.

CEMETERIES

Cemeteries are the summary of the human history of a town and stir the imagination of those who have the time and inclination to delve into the past. In the Wallingford Green Hill Cemetery, the Ives family plot with its wrought iron fence and corner decorations of marble lambs reflected the economic importance to nineteenth-century Vermont of the wool industry. Lent Ives' sheep probably pastured on the home farm just over the cemetery boundaries. But the wrought iron railings surrounding the Ives plot (and so many of the other family lots in Green Hill that at one time it was called the Cemetery of the Iron Fences) have not survived the wear and tear of the years.

This account attempts only to give general information regarding cemeteries in the township. It is based on a survey done for the Vermont Old Cemeteries Association under the direction of Stephen Maranville of East Wallingford. For some fifteen years, Mr. Maranville has been locating the smaller burial grounds no longer in use, and cleaning and repairing the stones, with the willing financial assistance of the Town Selectmen, from funds allotted them for this purpose.

The three largest cemeteries—Green Hill and St. Patrick's Catholic Cemeteries in Wallingford and Maple Grove in East Wallingford—are still in use and receiving excellent care. A number of years ago, Miss May L. Congdon compiled a card file for the West Hill, Hill or Roberts, Stafford, and Southard cemeteries in South Wallingford, and the Hagar, Hawkins, and Pelsue cemeteries in East Wallingford. This file, kept at the Town Clerk's office, is now the only record for many of the stones which were not graven to begin with, or are presently unreadable.

Green Hill Cemetery

In the village of Wallingford, on Route 7, at the southern edge of town. An attractive, well-kept cemetery which stretches up a hillside in terraces, from a pool and fountain at the left of the main entrance. The fountain and terraced levels led the Federal Writers' project in their

View from cemetery hill, Wallingford, by Birney Batcheller.

guide book on Vermont (1937) to comment that "the landscaping is such as to impart a slightly incongruous Versailles atmosphere."

The oldest section lies to the right of the center gate and contains some interesting late eighteenth-century headstones, including that of the Tory killed by Wallingford patriots in 1777 whose interment is said by Thorpe to be the reason for the cemetery. For the first hundred years this was the village burial ground and one finds family plots and names of the early area settlers in the older part near Main Street.

In 1870 the Green Hill Cemetery Association was formed and seventy-eight townspeople subscribed to the Association, to buy additional land for enlargement of the cemetery and for building a fence around it. Subscriptions ranged from $300 to $2.

The first officers and trustees elected that year (1870) were: President, Harvey Button; Vice-President, Alfred Hull; Clerk and Treasurer, E. W. Kent. The Trustees were John C. Batcheller, P. G. Clark, Hannibal Hopkins, William G. Marsh, I. B. Munson, John Scribner and C. M. Townsend.

The present By-Laws of the Association state that "This Association shall be composed of such persons as shall agree to the purposes of its constitution," and provide for an annual meeting and election of officers.

St. Patrick's Catholic Cemetery

Located east of the Green Hill Cemetery with its entrance on Church Street, in the village of Wallingford. The present cemetery, approximately 12 acres, came into the possession of the Roman Catholic Diocese in three stages:

1. August 15, 1873 by deed from Elias Kent, which included a right of way from Church Street to the land to be used for a burial ground. This section is to the west of the gate and is now referred to as the Old Section.

2. May 9, 1927 from Lucretia Kent Stone to the Diocese of Burlington, the section to the east of the entrance gate and the road leading from Church Street, now known as the New Section.

3. October 12, 1949 by deed from Sherwin Cootey to the Diocese of Burlington, land not yet cleared which is to the east and northeast of the New Section.

There is no clear indication as to the date of the first burial. At one time a Cemetery Association did exist with the late Mary Toohey as Treasurer. At the present time there are no members of the Association. All matters pertaining to the Cemetery are handled by the Pastor of St. Patrick's Church.

Maple Grove Cemetery

In the village of East Wallingford between Mill River and Route 103. The original cemetery, for which there are no records, occupied the top of the hill and its gravestones dating from the early and middle 1800's look down on Mill River and the village cross roads. In 1883 the Maple Grove Cemetery Association was organized with twelve charter members who elected as officers: President, Gilbert E. Johnson; Vice-President, T. R. Fuller; Secretary, Elisha Allen; Treasurer, A. H. Jackson. Its name comes from the maple trees set out at about that time by Jesse Wardwell and Henry Doty (the former, in his diary, mentions doing it and was then apparently in his late teens). The Association has enlarged the cemetery which now has several hundred graves and spreads down the east slope. A new section is being developed on land adjoining the north boundary.

Hawkins Family Cemetery

A family burial plot on the Hawkins farm a half mile north of Route 140, located beside the old county road from Wallingford to Mt. Holly, long unused, but whose track is still visible. The older part contains 13 graves of members of the Hawkins family, the earliest dating from 1815. All are relatives and descendants of Abraham Hawkins, one of the original Sugar Hill settlers, himself buried in the Sugar Hill Cemetery. There are also four small rough fieldstone markers whose identity and meaning are unknown although carefully tended by four generations of Hawkins. A new section, enclosed by a modern wire fence, was opened at the death of Maurice Hawkins in 1974. (The Hawkins family is presently the only one left, of the 27 farm families settled in the area 150 years ago, which is still actively farming.)

Hager Cemetery

A small family cemetery of about a dozen graves on the Wallach property not far from the Long Trail as it crosses north of Route 140. Its limits are marked by the remnants of stone walls which must have enclosed it. A marker names a German friend of the Wallachs whose ashes were brought here in 1948. The other stones are for the Bourn and Hager families and date from the early nineteenth century.

Pelsue Cemetery (Also known as Javary from previous owners of the land)

One mile south of Cuttingsville on Route 103. About 50 graves, including some with small local stones whose markings, if any, have long since worn away. All are nineteenth-century, the earliest date being 1816. Mrs. Javary remembers as a child on her way to school seeing bones being dug up by relatives for relocation in other cemeteries (today the front row is empty for that reason) and recalls her fear that there would be ghosts about.

Sugar Hill Cemetery

Three miles from East Wallingford on the Sugar Hill Road, which once ran through the center of an area originally farmed by twenty-seven families. A pleasant hillside graveyard kept in good condition and being gradually restored. Most of the 350 graves are nineteenth-century ones from the 27 families, and there is at least one Revolutionary soldier buried here. Eight graves of Civil War soldiers had been pinpointed and recently two more have been discovered and restored.

One of the last burials in the Sugar Hill Cemetery was in 1908. It was that of Delia Congdon, a deaf mute, whose pathetic story was local history in the first half of the twentieth century. Delia was beloved by all the Sugar Hill residents, especially by the school children who would often stop as they passed her house near the school to enjoy the milk and cookies which she always had ready for them. When she was 40 years old, she was murdered by Elroy Kent—it is said he used a shingle splitting knife—who had always been interested in her. It took authorities over a year to track down the murderer and during this time people on Sugar Hill locked their doors for the first time in their lives. Elroy Kent (not to be confused with the well-known botanist of the same name) was finally taken into custody in North Adams, Massachusetts, and hung. This is recorded as the last hanging in Vermont.

Doty Burying Ground

An early nineteenth-century graveyard located at the back of the Tuckaway Camp Grounds off Route 7 at South Wallingford. It was probably enclosed by stone walls as there are no signs of stone posts to which iron railings might have been fastened. Two of the several Revolutionary War soldiers in the town are buried here—Jerahmeel Doty, famed also as one of the body guard of 12 who escorted General Lafayette to France and returned with a loan to America of five million dollars, and Jonas Holden, who served at Bunker Hill and at Ticonderoga. Both were also soldiers in the War of 1812.

Hill or Roberts Cemetery

A carefully re-arranged burial ground of about 150 graves, of which only 10 have readable stones, situated out of sight on a hill above Route 7, a short distance below South Wallingford. Most of the weather beaten stones are crudely shaped from local fieldstone and all markings have been effaced by time and the cattle which have grazed here for many years. The only modern stone is that of the Hill family which bears data on the last burial in the cemetery in 1901.

Southard or Munson Cemetery

A tiny burial ground with only six gravestones so weather-beaten as to be completely blank. Located on the lane branching left where the Hartsboro Road turns south toward South Wallingford.

Stafford Cemetery

A small cemetery just off the Hartsboro Road where it turns north out of South Wallingford. Five Stafford graves with the dates of death ranging from 1856 to 1872; the sixth gravestone is that of a 12-year old boy named Albert Eddy who died in 1860. Granite posts lying about indicate an iron fence at some time.

West Hill Cemetery

A nineteenth-century graveyard no longer in use, although the Historic Records Survey for the Town of Wallingford, in its Inventory of 1941 listed it as still in use at that time. About two miles from South Wallingford on the West Hill Road, it is visible across a pasture where it lies on a low ridge sloping southwest. The entrance at the south end has a grilled-iron gate. There is also evidence from stone posts still in place, or lying about, that several of the family plots must have had iron railings. At the north end are a number of small native stone markers shaped as gravestones. These are set in burial arrangement, often grouped about a larger engraved family stone, but any markings or writings are long gone due to time and weathering. The most recent grave appears to be that of Benjamin Gorton who died in 1914.

Many of the handcarved headstones found in these cemeteries are probably the work of John R. Adair, proprietor of the Wallingford Monumental Works in the 1870's. He made and erected the stones; a favorite design was a dove.

Andrew Kull in his book on New England cemeteries finds the "most engaging stone" in the Green Hill Cemetery to be the one whose inscription begins, "Fell a victim to Death's cold hands on the 22nd of July 1812, Mr. Norman Towner / Ag'd 27 / one of societie's brightest ornaments. . ."

Sarah, wife of the famous Jerahmeel Doty, has the following verse: "Lo where the silent mail he weeps / A wife a friend a mother sleeps. . ."

A lugubrious verse on a West Hill stone says: "Man dieth and wasteth / Away yea man giveth up / The ghost and where is he. . ."

In contrast, an epitaph in Maple Grove says, "He always made home pleasant."

Chapter 9

Homes

WALLINGFORD

In tracing the history of homes in Wallingford village, one is struck by the number of houses, or parts of houses, which have been moved and made over for use at other sites. The Lent Ives house, built before 1800 where the Dunham house now stands, was moved to School Street, then it was moved back to make room for the new Town Hall (1906). Later it was refurbished, then was acquired by True Temper Inn for use of the hotel staff; now it is part of the English Language School property and serves as a student dormitory. The old town house that stood beside the Ives house on School Street was moved a short distance northeast to Taft Terrace, and used as a fire station; when the railroad station was converted to a fire station, the old one was made into a dwelling and is presently the Kenneth Reynolds home.

Two houses on Hull Avenue were ells taken off early Main Street houses. The Luella Ross house was part of the house of Zephaniah Hull at 18 North Main Street, and the house where Walter Wade now lives was the front part of the house at 15 North Main Street. A wing from the present Townsend house at 5 North Main Street was moved to the Creek Road and used as a dwelling. The most recent house-moving occurred at the former Scribner home at 41 South Main Street, now belonging to James and Lynn Gallipo. The rear part, a good-sized structure, was moved in 1974 to a site between its parent building and the Old Stone Shop, and now makes a separate and complete dwelling. The house at No. 49, farther down the street and next to the cemetery, once stood on the present site of the Goodyear Clark house; before being moved it was sawed in two so that, one is told, it could be brought across the bridge over Otter Creek.

In 1830, Judge Harvey Button built a house and law office on North Main Street next door to the Inn; the property remained in the family until 1961. His small law office burned in 1851 and was rebuilt in 1853; it was said to be the oldest such building in the state. In 1967, Mr. and Mrs. Gilbert from Dorset bought the Button property and moved the office to Dorset to be part of a reconstructed Colonial Village they were planning. They wanted to move the house also, but found that the cost of doing this was too much. For a time the house was rented to the Language Center for classrooms, and it was briefly a teen-age center. It is now owned by James and Sandra Marquis, who have an antique shop there.

Howard Harris home, now owned by James and Sandra Marquis

The Marquis home is next door at 10 North Main Street. In 1853, Howard Harris built and autographed this house on the site of his store, which had burned—the initials H. H. are in the slate of the roof. This was the boyhood home of Paul Harris, founder of Rotary International and grandson of Howard Harris. Originally the house was the standard square house with central stairway, with kitchen, pantry, and two wood sheds at the back. It has been considerably remodelled, and the barn torn down. For many years it was painted buff color with terra cotta trim because William C. Mason, the owner, admired that color scheme, which was always used on the Batcheller house across the street and the Batcheller Block on the nearby corner.

At 12 North Main Street is the house built in 1818 by Dr. John Fox, well-known medical practitioner; it is now owned by Hazel Hawkins Lawson. Much of the wood work is grain painted and still in excellent condition. In the kitchen a large old fireplace, warming oven, and old soapstone sink give evidence of the period in which it was built. In the back part of the house, a four-hole privy was recently removed to make a closet for the apartment now located in the rear. For many years Mrs. Lawson was the local seamstress, and there were few homes in

Wallingford or Clarendon where she did not go to make the ladies new summer or winter gowns. In many places she would stay several days, and sleep at night in the cold guest-room feather bed.

The house at 16 North Main, where the Weeks family lives, has been called the "upside down" house because the ceilings upstairs are higher than those downstairs. At the time this house was built, the procedure was to lay the timbers on the ground and frame them for the bottom section and the top section of the house. Then a crew of men would be gotten together to raise these sections and fasten them in place. It is said that those who did the raising were addled by too much hard cider, or whatever they had to support their efforts, and put the top sections on the foundation and the bottom and taller section on top.

A few houses down and across the street at No. 25 is the house now known as the Congdon Funeral Home. The business was started by Lyman Congdon in 1910. Dr. John Miller and H. B. Barden walked up the railroad tracks to Clarendon to the home farm where Lyman and his family were visiting to ask him to locate in Wallingford, knowing that he had worked in a funeral establishment in Albany, New York.

As for the house itself, it was once known as "Marm Hull's Tavern." The cellar has hand-hewn beams, and the upstairs rooms still have latches and long hinges. Several of the rooms have visible corner posts, and plank walls were discovered when it came to installing modern electricity and insulation. The wide floors have long been covered with hard wood flooring. About 1949, when the front porch was to be removed and a front walk put down, a locust tree had to be cut; when the stump of the tree was pulled out, a Spanish coin was found bearing the words "Hispaniarum Rex" and the date 1721 on one side, and "Philippus" on the other. The coin still remains in the possession of the family.

Returning along the west side of North Main Street, we come to the home of Harold and Helen Weidman at No. 11. Its history typifies the many changes in ownership which have occurred with some of these older homes. On April 12, 1810, Augustus Milford deeded 32 rods of ground to William Fox, Jr., brother of Dr. John Fox, for sixty dollars. Some time between 1810 and 1817 William built a house and barn on this lot, and on January 15, 1818, he sold the property to Daniel Robarts. Then between 1818 and 1964 this property changed hands by sale or inheritance some 17 times. The purchase price on July 23, 1846 was $550. In 1924 the appraised value was $1500 when it was inherited by Birney Batcheller as a part of his mother's estate. The present owners purchased the property in 1964.

On Hillside Avenue, off upper School Street, is the home of Sherwin and Leona Fish. The ranch-type house sits on a hill overlooking the village. Mr. Fish, a building contractor, started construction in 1965,

Sherwin and Leona Fish home

and the house was completed in 1973. The exterior is brown-stained vertical siding, faced on the east side with Vermont mica schist stone from the Gassetts area. The house, heated by electricity, consists of nine rooms, three baths, and a two-car attached garage. There is also a separate shop. The house has large expanses of glass. A floor-to-ceiling fireplace in the sunken living room is constructed from the Gassetts mica stone. Of special interest are the hand-hewn beams in the family room ceiling; these came from the present fire station, which was originally the old railroad station. The handmade bricks in the family room fireplace came from an old house in Wells, Vermont, and are about 175 years old.

Returning down School Street, we come to the home of Fred and Lois Thurlow, at No. 12 across from the Town Hall. They have maintained and improved this old home, believed to have been built by D. E. Nicholson in 1865. The fine maple trees which used to stand in front were casualties of the widening of School Street in the 1960's. Its water supply came from a spring of clear cold water on the former Kelley farm, which also supplied the Hotel, Odd Fellows Block, Library, and a number of residences; recently this was changed over to village water.

In addition to being a residence, 12 School Street has been the home of several businesses. Mrs. Winifred Saunders, whose parents had purchased the property in 1875, had the first telephone office here. She was Town Clerk and Treasurer from 1922 to 1938, and performed the duties of that office, including the issuing of marriage licenses and administering the Freeman's Oath, here in her home. Fred Thurlow now has his real estate office here (Thurlow and Nash).

Our next stop is at the Dunham house, No. 7 on the east side of South Main Street. In 1856, Isaac Bradley Munson built this, the first Victorian house in the village, to retire to from his farm on the Hartsboro Road, now occupied by Warren Baker. His farm was a red brick Colonial with fireplaces, but Isaac wanted stoves, and so his new "town house" had a hole for a stovepipe in every room except the parlor, which had a fireplace. Subsequent owners have kept it that way and have made no significant changes in the original construction. The ceilings are twelve feet high and the house is insulated by being "double-lathed and back-plastered." The foundation is of tooled marble lined with red brick. The barn has a pacing-horse weather vane. Horace Earl, a son-in-law of Isaac Munson, used to race pacing horses at the race track in South Wallingford.

In all of its 120 years there have been but four owners. One of these was Mrs. Malina Hodges, whom everyone called "Aunt Mynie." She

Isaac Bradley Munson home, now owned by Beatrice Dunham

lived there alone until she was ninety-four. Professor and Mrs. Dunham bought the house in 1934 at an auction to settle the estate. They used it only in the summer for the next 17 years until they moved to Wallingford in 1956. They have kept the home decorated and furnished in a Victorian style appropriate to its architecture, that of the first Victorian house to be built in Wallingford.

Farther down South Main Street and to the left on Church Street is Mrs. Natalie MacIntyre's house. Not much is known about its history, other than that it is an old house that has been "modernized" inside several times, and that it was once the home of Miss May Congdon, for many years Librarian at Gilbert Hart Library; she died in a fire which badly damaged the building.

When the MacIntyres acquired it, Mrs. MacIntyre reports that "the house had seven rooms, but two of the four upstairs bedrooms were rather like closets, no windows. There were no closets in the house at all. The upstairs slanted seven inches from east to west walls . . . someone had hoped to "modernize" the house, so had installed Victorian windows . . . cutting studs (which had caused sagging) . . . and had removed the central fireplace. . . . Insofar as the interior walls were concerned, they were exceedingly patched and rough." There were so many things to be remedied that the whole interior was gutted and then reconstructed. A wing was built on the north side which has a bedroom and bath above and a kitchen, utility room, and bath below. The house is now an attractive and livable six-room house, not "authentic," but it was even less "authentic" when the MacIntyres bought it.

The Ward home, a brick house at 47 South Main, called by some a three-fourths New England Colonial, was probably built around 1825. The wooden ell was added later. Perry Wells started the first bakery in town there. It was only a shell of a house, but "a very nice shell," when Mrs. Clarence Ward bought it in 1907. It has been modernized for comfortable living without changing the general structure. For a time the four fireplaces, one of which has a brick oven, were sealed but now are open and usable.

Farther down the street and two houses beyond the cemetery is the property often referred to as the "Hopkins Farm." The house is now occupied by the new owners, Dr. and Mrs. DeSilvey and their children. The original house was built in 1784 by Benjamin Bradley and his son, Daniel. It was probably constructed as a hip-roof central-chimney house, and modified around 1800-1820 into a traditional gable-roof double-chimney structure. In the mid-1800's, or a bit later, the double chimneys were removed when the fireplaces were replaced by wood stoves.

In 1899, Hadwin Hopkins purchased the farm and devoted the rest of his life to farming. His sons, Ernest and Rob, went to Boston to earn their fortunes in the trolley car business. Ernest stayed there and Rob returned to manage the family farm. As the family fortunes improved, the house was changed; hardwood floors, a new chimney and furnace, and a new front porch were added. The old porch is the present side porch of the Clifford Willard house. Following Rob's death, the next owner, Hugh Young, extensively restored the interior, leaving the original floor plan unchanged. The Youngs also removed the large front porch, returning the facade to its original Colonial simplicity.

Just beyond and in back of the De Silveys, on land once part of the Hopkins Farm, is the Youngs' new house. This was built in 1975 by Lee Houghton, a local builder, and stands among second-growth hardwoods on the lower slopes of Green Hill. The house is designed for low maintenance care both inside and out. The exterior is vertical rough-sawn cedar from Western Canada. Because of the energy situation, the interior has three separate areas for flexibility in heating control. There are high cathedral ceilings in the living room and bedrooms upstairs, and a careful use of glass and a skylight, permitting effective solar ex-

Hugh and Carolyn Young home

posure. Open plank stairs lead to a balcony which has a uniquely designed railing of redwood and steel bars. Many of the fixtures are interesting adaptations of older objects, such as an old hanging lamp from over a kitchen table now lighting the stair landing, its wrought iron chain from the old Hopkins Farm; wrought iron hardware on cupboards and bookcases; and original lamps from an old carriage which function as outdoor lights. An attached garage and small greenhouse are a part of this completely contemporary house.

The Bogerts—Maple Lane Farm, Haven Hill Road

In 1780, Titus Andrews bought this property from Isaac Hall, and it changed hands several times by purchase and inheritance over the years. For a time it was called the Lane Farm; Bertha Lane, now Mrs. Bertha Savery, lived there as a child. It was noted for its sugar bush, from which, it was said, a very fine grade of maple syrup was produced. In 1952, the Bogerts bought the farm from the Elmer Carrs, who had made many changes in the house. The original kitchen was turned into a living room, the fireplace was pushed back to the north wall, and the old hand-hewn beams were left exposed in the ceiling. The Bogerts added a large enclosed porch at the back, the floor tiled with pink marble from a bank that was dismantled.

The Kellys—Goodyear Clark House, Route 7 South

This 15-room house of Greek Revival architecture was built by P. Goodyear Clark in 1845 on a 250-acre farm. In 1943 the farm was still owned by his direct descendants. Until 1970 it remained intact as a farm, although it changed hands several times during that period.

For many years the Clarks operated a summer boarding house— Maple Grove Farm—for vacationing guests, who would stay as long as six weeks, many returning year after year. The family would move to the third floor so that their guests could have the second floor rooms. The large dining room held several tables seating four, and a large center table seating eight. The strong gravity feed from a spring located two miles back of the house provided water for sinks in the second and third floor halls. The Clark family is believed to have operated the first roadside stand in Vermont, where their own maple products and jellies, along with ice cream and other snacks, were sold.

Walter and Nancy Kelly acquired the property in 1970, and until 1974 they operated a guest house in partnership with Mr. and Mrs. Thomas Murray (Mr. Kelly's sister). "The Inn Place" as it was then called, offered eight rooms and had similar dining facilities to the earlier guest house. The guests then were attracted mostly by the fall foliage and winter skiing.

The McCarthys—Israel Munson Farm

This handsome wooden house, on Route 7 where the Hartsboro Road turns off, was the home farm of Israel Munson (1808-1887) and was one of the farms included in the trust he established to provide for his two sons. In 1933, the executors sold this farm to Arthur and Maud Davison. The Davisons, and later their son Howard and his wife Marguerite, operated it as a dairy farm until 1972, when it was sold to real estate brokers. In March, 1973, they sold it to James and Joanne McCarthy, and now it is again for sale.

The Ketchams—Isaac Munson (1771-1835) Farm, Route 7 South

Israel Munson came to Wallingford in October, 1804, and purchased a farm for his brother Isaac. (Isaac Bradley Munson and the younger Israel Munson were Isaac's sons.) Probably some time around 1830, Isaac replaced the wood frame building, which he and his family first lived in, with a handsome brick house. It is said that the different brick patterns on the front and back were the work of two masons with different ideas.

In 1933 this farm was purchased by Thomas and Elizabeth Ketcham and operated as a dairy farm for many years until Mr. Ketcham's recent retirement. It is still their home, and maintained with loving attention to its architectural and historical features.

The Gilmans, General Robinson Hall House

Isaac Munson's oldest daughter, Sarah, married General Robinson Hall. This house, of red brick, was built for them about 1814. It is situated on the west side of Route 7 about a mile north of South Wallingford, and from the outside resembles the home of the Ketchams. It is presently occupied by Mr. and Mrs. John B. Gilman, who have lived there since 1948. It too has been maintained with thought and care both inside and out.

The Chases, Hartsboro Road

The John Chase home, which they acquired in 1970, is on the Hartsboro Road at the corner where a branch road formerly went to Sugar Hill, but now goes only part way. Samuel Townsend bought the property in 1852. This was the general location of the hamlet of Hartsboro; records of that time mention a schoolhouse on the southeast corner of the property, and a sawmill lot across the road and to the north; also there are a number of cellar holes in the area. Owners since Townsend include James Patch, remembered for the barn dances and kitchen hops held here when he had the place, and Ben and Viola Hutchinson, who

General Robinson Hall home, now owned by John and Harriet Gilman

bought the property in 1946 and remodelled it, naming it Merry Brook. Beavers at work in the brook probably developed the pond presently east from the house, and also may have caused the swampy condition of the former schoolhouse site.

SOUTH WALLINGFORD

Houses in the outlying areas have changed more since early days than those in the village itself. On West Hill, some of the farm houses are being used as retirement homes. The former West Hill schoolhouse was for a time a vacation home, but is now used year round. There are a number of new and remodelled homes east of Otter Creek, on the East and Hartsboro Roads.

On Route 7 near the Danby line is the relatively new home of long-time Town Representative Ralph Stafford. It contrasts with the home of his brother Guy next door, which is one of the oldest in the area. This eleven-room house was purchased by Boardman Stafford, grandfather of the present generation, in 1878, from William Croft; Guy Stafford inherited it from his father, Dwight Stafford, in 1937. The house was owned by Quakers in 1867, and was used as a Quaker meetinghouse for a few years. It is supposed to have been an almshouse before that. When the house was built is not known, but early records indicate that Stutely Stafford purchased it from Chrispin Bull in 1796.

The Stanford Taylors—The Rogers Farm, West Hill

In 1968 the parcel of land on West Hill lying within the boundaries of both Tinmouth and Wallingford and known as the "old Rogers Farm" was purchased by Stanford and Dorothea Taylor of Long Island, New York. Previous owners of this parcel, from the Rogers forward, were Robert and Orba Beer, Rudolf and Rose Chaval and the Maggards.

During much of its existence, the Rogers parcel was operated both as a family farm and as a country inn to which guests came in the summer to enjoy views of Danby and Dorset Mountains, and to relax under the butternut and maple trees in the yard. For several years after it ceased offering overnight accommodations, the Rogers house was celebrated for the delicious dinner that was served there on Sunday afternoons.

When the Taylors had the house reconstructed and restored, they retained the lines of the former structure—cleaning and strengthening the beams and stonework that formed part of the dining room that is so much remembered by many people in Wallingford.

The corn crib that had stood for years near the east side of the house was removed, as was a shed at the back door.

The Taylors have added to the original Rogers parcel the piece of land that is adjacent to West Hill cemetery and which is traversed by the remains of the former coach road to Tinmouth. The woodlands still bear vestiges of those who lived in or passed through them long ago.

EAST WALLINGFORD

The box-type house was popular in East Wallingford in the early days, because it was easy to build and required the least amount of wood. The residence of James and Katherine McCann on the Sugar Hill Road was originally such a one when it was built about 120 years ago. Another old house, beyond theirs, dates from the early 1800's and once belonged to the late Dennis McCann, Sr.

There are several old houses in the village. One known as the "gable house" stands on School Street across from the post office. The

Ashley Graves home, now owned by Roland Seward

home now owned by Mr. and Mrs. Stanley Seward across the road from the Seward farm house is another. The 1927 flood took half of the oldest, owned at that time by Warren Cole; the part that was left has now been rebuilt. Although it was decided that the house and farm were in Mt. Holly, the address has not been changed and is still East Wallingford.

Houses erected by Orvis McKnight in the 19th century still stand on School Street, but have been remodelled and modernized. The one he built for Ashley Graves was typical Victorian, ornate inside and out. His own, next to it, was supposed to be the same but was never completed in as elaborate a style. A third was a huge ark, built for a doctor, complete with an office with its own entrance.

Hawkins Farmhouse

Five generations of the Hawkins family have operated the Hawkins farm, north of Route 140 and up the hill. The site offers a beautiful view of the countryside. Abraham Hawkins started the first farmhouse, a log cabin, February 24, 1798; it was replaced by a frame house on the site of the present sugar house. The existing house, the third, was built about 130 years ago. It is a two family house of good size; Edgar Hawkins, of the fifth generation lives in one side, his mother in the other.

Chapter 10
Notable Events and Landmarks

"World's Fair"
Wallingford Pageant
Town Hall
Community Christmas Tree
Wedding Gown Tea
Wallingford Summer Festival

Wallingford Bicentennial
Fishing Derbies
The Old Covered Bridge
White Rocks
Boy with the Boot

"WORLD'S FAIR"

A fair, called the "World's Fair" was held annually at South Wallingford from 1891 until July, 1960, on land leased from Roy Stafford. This was an ideal location because it was near the railroad track and there was a hill on the west side of the property which made a natural grandstand. From the hillside, patrons could get a fine view of the horse races on the half mile track close by. One of the thoroughbreds which raced there and "won many a purse" was "Belle B," owned by M. H. Roberts. Sponsor of the Fair was the Union Park Driving Society.

South Wallingford Fair

The following is quoted from a newspaper article dated 1909.

"Better horses are coming than have ever been here for the races. . . . Midway will have more than its usual attractions in addition to the inevitable merry-go-round, Ferris wheel, strikers, throwers, etc. . . . The ladies promise a good showing for the floral hall. . . . Good cattle, sheep, swine, poultry, etc. are expected. Little Ruth, the smallest horse in the world, will be one of the attractions which are too numerous to mention in detail. A good band, perhaps two, will try to harmonize and equalize the atmosphere, and if the weather clerk prove in good humor the fair will prove a rousing one, with crowds of people. Go and help swell the bunch."

WALLINGFORD PAGEANT—1912

Members of the Committee appointed to arrange a "safe and sane" Fourth of July celebration in 1912 were Rev. Walter Thorpe, W. P. Cary, H. G. Savery, Rev. T. J. Henry, A. W. Ferguson, A. G. Stone, and Wm. C. Mason. Inspired by the success of the 1911 pageant (which is described at length in Thorpe's History), the Committee decided to have another Historical Pageant, this one to portray important events of early American History. This Pageant also took place at the natural amphitheatre in the woods bordering on Elfin Lake.

The opening scene showed the "Coming of the Norsemen." Battle axes in hand, they sprang from their boat, which had shields along its side. After exploring the land and finding grapes, they named it "Vineland."

The second scene was of the American Indian before the white man came. More than 50 people participated in this one scene. Indian sports and pastimes were shown, along with skill in hunting and phases of communal life.

Then followed the coming of Columbus in his flagship, the Santa Maria. The players in this scene wore 15th century costumes, carried Spanish flags, and claimed the land in the name of the Queen of Spain.

Champlain's discovery of the lake which bears his name was enacted in the fourth scene. He and two white companions were accompanied by Algonquin Indians to the edge of the lake, and there were attacked by a band of Iroquois. When fired upon, the Iroquois, who had never heard or seen gunfire, fled in confusion and terror.

The early life of New England was then represented, in the customs and practices of the Puritans. The courtship of Miles Standish and Priscilla, and the taking of one accused of witchcraft, who was placed in a ducking stool and submerged in the lake, were enacted at each performance.

Life in New Amsterdam showed the influence of the Dutch in the settlement of our country, and was enlivened by Governor Stuyvesant with a real wooden leg. There was trading with the Indians and singing and dancing, including that of little Dutch girls.

The culmination of the Pageant portrayed the enthronement of Peace (Columbia), symbolized by a young lady, accompanied by two friends, all dressed in flowing Grecian costumes and guarded by the hopes of the future (Young America). Then followed all who had taken part in the Pageant, grouped before and below the figure of Peace.

Free tickets were given every student in the Wallingford schools, and also those in Rutland and neighboring towns. Money left over after paying all expenses was given to the School Building Committee for the purpose of installing hygenic drinking fountains in the school building.

TOWN HALL

"The new town hall which was opened last Wednesday evening with the third annual "Old Folks" dance, is a fine structure, and adds materially to the attractions of this place. Nearly 200 people were present at the opening, including many from Rutland and surrounding towns. The function has become a popular one and the event was especially notable this year in connection with the opening of the building. The Stafford-Mellow orchestra furnished music and supper was served by White Rock Rebekah Lodge, being prepared in the new kitchen and dining room." (From the *Rutland Herald* of December 5, 1906.)

Money for construction of the town hall was provided by gifts and loans from Alphonzo P. Stafford and Alonzo Kent, and for the town clock by gift from Joseph Randall. It quickly became the central spot of activity for all occasions. Many graduations, dances, plays, movies—all took place here. Public affairs were settled at the Hall and lively Town Meetings were annual occurrences. However, at a special Town Meeting in June 1973, it was voted to close the upstairs to public meetings. Town Meetings, and other large gatherings formerly held there, now take place in the Elementary School.

The jail for the town was in the basement. Many a tramp had overnight lodging and a light meal there over the years. It was so used until 1960 when the jail was removed and a youth center was started and flourished for several years under the guidance of School authorities.

The Town Clerk's offices now occupy the right side of the first floor. The large, well-lighted main office with its big front and side windows is familiar to town taxpayers, license seekers and the various and sundry citizenry having dealings with town government.

A fireproof door and metal shelving for the vault, which were required for the safe keeping of Town records in case of fire, were donated by Mr. and Mrs. Bert McClure. These were installed in August 1971 and dedicated to Mrs. Bertha Savery in recognition of her 23 years of town service. The old door was given to Tinmouth whose town fathers were very appreciative of the gift.

Town Hall

THE COMMUNITY CHRISTMAS TREE

A special event which flourished in Wallingford early in the twentieth century was its Community Christmas Tree. An account in the December 1913 issue of *The Vermonter* gives the Rev. Walter Thorpe much of the credit for encouraging and aiding this "milestone" in celebrating the Yuletide, and applauds the "example set by energetic little Wallingford."

Several days before Christmas a group of volunteers would bring a large evergreen from the woods and erect it, trimmed with red and green lights, on the side lawn of the hotel, now the English Language Center. At that time there was no shrubbery along the street sides.

Evidently the evening program began with a children's hour of singing and stereoptican views "thrown upon a huge screen suspended from trees not far from The Tree," to quote from Adele Duval's article in *The Vermonter*. At ten o'clock the carollers appeared. They too sang and saw "stereoptican views of a highly educational nature, whose worthiness was intensified and more duly appreciated because of the explanatory lectures by Mr. Thorpe."

After refreshments and a rehearsal of hymns, the carollers set out at midnight to "chant in harmonious unison in the principal streets and near the homes of the sick and convalescent, anthems of Christmas-tide." Miss Duval also mentions the snow fall the day before the 1913 celebration, which added to the "splendor of the scene" and seems to have led to a snow-ball scrimmage which sent everyone home in a merry mood.

WEDDING GOWN TEA

The Wedding Gown Tea, held at the home of Mrs. Minnie Stafford Klock, was a fund raising project for the Congregational Church that became a community affair. The following account was taken from an article which appeared in the *Rutland Herald* of August 24, 1931.

"Wallingford, Aug. 23. About 250 people thronged the grounds of the A. P. Stafford house this afternoon and evening for the Wedding Gown Tea given by the summer residents headed by Mrs. Philip Whitehead and Mrs. R. C. Spencer. All the neighboring towns were well represented, especially Rutland, Clarendon, Pittsford, Danby, and Pawlet.

"Tea and supper were served on tables in the yard under the old elm trees. There was a fire in the great fireplace in the old kitchen. Mrs. Laura Scribner, in a gown of nearly a century ago, and her grandaughter, Miss Phyllis Warner of Wayne, Pa., sat knitting beside it. In the opposite corner Mrs. Moxley was spinning wool on an old spinning wheel.

"The procession of brides came down the front stairway into the yard and encircled the house, to stand in a receiving line on the south side. Most of the older wedding gowns were of colored silk, satin, or velvet." There were 42 brides in line, and the gowns they wore dated from 1931 back to the early 1800's.

WALLINGFORD SUMMER FESTIVAL

An event which highlighted summer activity in Wallingford during the 50's became widely known throughout Vermont as the Wallingford Summer Festival, and for several years was regularly listed in *Vermont Life* among its annual summer events.

The Reverend Thomas H. Connor, pastor of St. Patrick's Church, was the individual whose concern resulted in the Festival. He saw a new school being built and was thoroughly disappointed when he learned that it was to be equipped with the furnishings (desks, chairs, etc.) from the old school. Some of that equipment was said to be 65 years old in 1953. He talked with Waldo W. White, then he and Waldo talked with Ralph W. Congdon. They took their story to others, and this resulted in a meeting at the Town Hall on the evening of May 9, 1953. The Citizens' Committee formed that evening under the chairmanship of David H. Eaton, with Father Connor as Vice-Chairman, sent out a letter expressing the Committee's ideas and objectives.

"We plan to contact everyone who is interested in our youngsters, our schools, and our town; its welfare and its possibilities. Many of the alumni of Wallingford Schools have made good in the business and industrial world and are in a position to help tremendously with this project. Our summer residents have often expressed the desire to help with some worthwhile project if they knew how. This will be their opportunity. Others, who are not financially able to contribute to the project will be given a chance to work for its success.

"To start the ball a-rolling, we are planning a Fair. . . ."

The idea for a Street Fair was given to the Committee by Rufus E. Brown. He guided its development. It was an idea which caught on at once; its time had come.

The first Street Fair was held on July 24 and 25, 1953. The original committees, numbering 26, drew helpers like magnets, so that within three weeks the whole town was working. Each group, with its chosen activity, carried its own ball with complete devotion and dependability.

The first Festival in 1953, held in excellent weather, netted over $3300. Of this sum, $3100 was paid toward the purchase of new desks and other equipment in time for the September 1953 opening of the school. A group of local businessmen signed a note for over $2000 to cover the balance due on these school furnishings. In 1954, the weather was less favorable, but the same community spirit carried through and enough was earned to pay off the note.

Succeeding Festivals in the 50's supported various community projects such as stage equipment and decoration for the Town Hall, an Industrial Arts course, a playground on the Ainsworth lot, Little League, the Girl Scouts, the Library, and others. By the 60's, changing times and needs were reflected in a lessening of the total community involvement and projects. In its annual listing of summer events in 1964, *Vermont Life* for the first time calls it the Wallingford Summer Smorgasbord. The popular smorgasbord supper, always an important part of the earlier festivals, became eventually its only remaining feature. Under the capable direction of Thelma Perry, supper chairman from 1954 to the final summer smorgasbord in the early 70's, a varied menu was served to hundreds of Wallingfordians, tourists, and visitors.

WALLINGFORD'S BICENTENNIAL YEAR 1761-1961

Wallingford celebrated its Bicentennial July 28 and 29, 1961. Friday there was a tour of 16 homes which were opened to the public, and their history told by their present owners. Two gardens, those of Mrs. R. C. Taft and Mrs. G. A. Wiedenmayer, were also open, and eight public buildings. Punch and cookies were served at the Gilbert Hart Library.

The First Selectman of Wallingford, Connecticut, and his wife were entertained by local Town officials, and on Saturday afternoon a cable call was received from the Mayor of Wallingford, England. Pictures of the Mayor and his wife, and newspapers, were later received by the Town Clerk; the newspapers gave a detailed account of the transatlantic conversation, which had excited much interest in the English city. A tape recording of this historic event was made, and played at another bicentennial program held here in the fall.

A sumptuous Smorgasbord supper served both evenings at the Elementary School by the Summer Festival Committee climaxed the celebration.

The Town officers provided information to the *Rutland Herald* for its special issue of September 6, 1961, describing the settlement and growth of Rutland County towns, Wallingford among them. The Library has a copy of that special issue on file.

The final celebration of the Bicentennial Year took place at the Town Hall on November 26, the anniversary eve of the signing of Wallingford's charter. James Cassel read the charter, and others spoke of Wallingford's history and its future. Descendants of some of Wallingford's early settlers were introduced. The recording of the transatlantic conversation made in July was played. Music was under the direction of Mrs. Ralph Lidstone, and included songs by a sextet from the High School and the singing of *America the Beautiful* by the audience at the close.

FISHING DERBIES

In the years 1972, 1973, 1974 and 1975 Sherwin W. and Leona B. Fish held fishing derbies at their pond at their home in Wallingford for children up to 15 years of age from Wallingford, Clarendon, Mt. Holly and Tinmouth. In the years 1972 and 1973 the pond was stocked with trout by Sherwin Fish. The State of Vermont Fish and Game Department, interested in fishing derbies for children, furnished the trout in 1974 and 1975. In 1972 money for prizes was donated by Wallingford businesses. The succeeding years prizes were furnished by the Fishes.

During the four years the number of children participating ranged from 50 to 119. The largest number of trout caught was 178, in 1975. The largest trout was a 19½" rainbow caught by four-year old Jeff Davenport of Wallingford in 1975.

Wallingford friends aided in registering the children, measuring the trout, and cooking and serving refreshments.

THE OLD COVERED BRIDGE

The covered bridge across Otter Creek was built in 1875 by Nicholas Powers of Clarendon. At a special Town meeting in October, 1874, it had been voted to build a new road from Wallingford village near the depot to Tinmouth, and about where the present Route 140 is. The necessary money for surveying and building the road and bridge was to be raised by a tax on the grand list.

In 1949 the old bridge was declared unsafe by the Highway Commissioner and had to be torn down. This was done in June of that year. Metal from the roof was used at the old Jennings school, where town equipment was stored, and some of the timbers were sold. Many people were sorry to see the bridge dismantled; they rescued wooden pegs and old square spikes and carried them away as souvenirs. The rest of the bridge was burned at the site. Remnants left were collected and piled at the corner of Batcheller Field, and then added to a bonfire which followed the Halloween parade.

Looking south over the Mill Pond to the Covered Bridge and the Ice House, by Birney Batcheller

WHITE ROCKS

The most spectacular and enduring landmark in the town is the cliff and huge slide of boulders on the face of the mountain known as White Rocks. Edwin L. Bigelow, in an article obtained from the U. S. Forest Service, states: "The cause of the slide and the date of its occurrence will probably never be known," but he concludes that it must have happened many thousand, and probably a million or more years ago. That this bare slide has not been covered with vegetation is most unusual. Mr. Bigelow attributes this to the fact that the rock is quartzite and so hard that the ages of weathering have failed to provide enough soil to sustain plant life.

The "Ice Beds" are beneath the huge boulders at the base of the slide. From there a "stream of ice cold water emerges along with a current of cold air, and ice is said to be found deep among the boulders as late as August. Snow during the winter seeps so deeply into crevices that the sun never reaches it, or the warm outside air either."

One of the numerous legends concerning White Rocks, related in Hager's "Economical Geology of Vermont (1862)" tells about a "money cave." An elderly Spaniard, befriended by a Vermonter from Chester, tells him the secret of a rich silver mine buried beneath a great slide of rocks. But despite many attempts to blast out the slide of rocks, says Hager, the rich lode of silver has never been reached.

THE BOY WITH THE BOOT

The Boy with the Boot fountain, erected in 1898, was given in memory of Arnold Hill by his children. Mr. Hill, a farmer and merchant, came to Wallingford with his family in the early 1850's. During the Civil War years and until his wife's health failed, he was landlord of the inn. He sold the inn around 1870; later he bought a farm on upper School Street and built the farmhouse, now the home of John Blanchard, where he spent the rest of his life.

Family tradition says the design is similar to a fountain in a Chicago park near where one of the Hill sons lived. Although extensive research has been done by a number of people, apparently no one has discovered who the original sculptor was, or when the first Boy with the Boot was erected. There are a number of similar statues around the country, and correspondence about one or another of them occasionally comes to the Library.

The original gift was to the school, and the school directors took responsibility for its care. But for some years it was forgotten or considered superfluous, for when Harry Clark came to the hotel as manager around 1920, he found it stored in the attic. The statue was put back in its place. Its basin, a watering trough for horses, first stood at the side of the road near the corner, then was moved to the lawn of the Inn after widening of Route 7. Around 1950, it was left too late in the fall, and was frozen into a solid chunk of ice. After that, because it is connected to the village water system, it was turned over to the Prudential Committee for care.

The statue has been damaged several times and is difficult to repair because it is made of zinc, not bronze as has been reported, and cannot be welded. Some years ago it was given a coat of aluminum paint to brighten up the dull zinc finish. In more recent years the boy has been painted in more lifelike colors, which are renewed each spring when the statue is brought out of winter storage. It is of special interest to children, who in this age of automobiles have to be told of its original use. For years it has been, and it still is, a notable landmark on the main street of Wallingford village.

Boy with the Boot, by Donald Wiedenmayer

BIBLIOGRAPHY

People of Wallingford. BIRNEY C. BATCHELLER. Stephen Daye Press. Brattleboro, Vermont, 1937.

History of Wallingford, Vermont. WALTER THORPE. The Tuttle Company. Rutland, Vermont, 1911.

Town of Wallingford. Annual Reports and Old Records.

Inventory of Town, Village, and City Archives of Vermont. Volume XXV, Town of Wallingford—The Historical Records Survey, Montpelier, Vermont, 1941.

Rutland Daily Herald. News items from old issues.

Vermont Tradition. DOROTHY CANFIELD FISHER. Little, Brown & Company. Boston, Mass., 1953.

Agricultural Trends in Wallingford, Vermont. The Agricultural Extension Service, University of Vermont and State Agricultural College. Burlington, Vermont, 1939.

History of Rutland County, Vermont. H. P. SMITH & W. S. RANN. D. Mason & Company. Syracuse, New York, 1886.

Atlas of Rutland County, Vermont. F. W. BEERS, 1869. Charles E. Tuttle Company. Rutland, Vermont, 1969.

Gazetteer of the State of Vermont. ZADOCK THOMPSON, A.B. E. P. Walton, Printer. Montpelier, Vermont, 1824.

Vermont Historical Gazetteer. ABBY MARIA HEMINGWAY. Claremont Manufacturing Company. 1877.

Gazetteer and Business Directory of Rutland County, Vermont for 1881-82. Hamilton Child, Syracuse, N. Y., 1881.

Rutland Suburban Directory, 1911. H. A. Manning Company, Springfield, Mass.

Vermont—A Guide to the Green Mountain State. American Guide Series —Federal Writers Project of WPA Administration for the State of Vermont. Houghton Mifflin. 1937.

Vermont Under Four Flags—A History of the Green Mountain State 1635-1975. PERRY H. MERRILL, Author and Publisher. Montpelier, Vermont, 1975.

New England Cemeteries—A Collectors Guide. ANDREW KULL. The Stephen Greene Press, Brattleboro, Vermont, 1974.

Vermont Yearbook. The National Survey, Chester, Vermont. Various years.

The First Congregational Church of Wallingford, Vermont, Inc. A Review of the First One Hundred and Fifty Years. MRS. EDMUND N. EDGERTON. 7/26/42.

Vermont Life - Summer 1968, Fall 1953. Agency of Development and Community Affairs, Montpelier, Vermont.